ZAP
THE
GAPS!

ZAP
THE
GAPS!

Target Higher
Performance and Achieve It!

Ken Blanchard
Dana Robinson
Jim Robinson

WILLIAM MORROW
An Imprint of HarperCollins*Publishers*

HarperCollins books may be purchased for educational, business, or sales promotional use. For information please write: Special Markets Department, HarperCollins Publishers Inc., 10 East 53rd Street, New York, NY 10022.

FIRST EDITION

Designed by Nancy Singer Olaguera

Printed on acid-free paper

Library of Congress Cataloging-in-Publication Data has been applied for.

ISBN 0-06-050300-9

02 03 04 05 06 ❖/RRD 10 9 8 7 6 5 4 3 2 1

To readers in every kind of organization who are committed to zapping what "is" in order to attain what "should be"

CONTENTS

FOREWORD

*T*here are magic moments in each of our lives. For me these have included: my six-year-old daughter running toward me, arms flung wide, with delighted screams of, "Daddy! Daddy!"; sitting quietly with my wife watching ducklings paddle in the marsh grass; listening to Beethoven's "Ode to Joy"; seeing my son, suddenly a man, stride across the stage and receive his law degree. All these moments, and many more, are perfect. Perfect because there is no gap between what is, and what should be.

But the real story of our lives as parents, spouses, employers, or employees often revolves around our quest to zap the gaps we perceive between where we are and where we think we should be.

Now, imagine a workplace where the reality of what employees do every day matches exactly what they should be doing. No gaps to zap. Exciting thought, isn't it? All, too often, though, the reality is just the opposite. Gaps abound.

This is exactly the challenge my friend Ken Blanchard and his colleagues Dana and Jim Robinson tackle in this book. Through a simple story, they show how two managers faced with a job-threatening situation discover how to dig down to the real core of the problem in the department, and then how they follow a step-by-step plan to zap the gaps. The process we learn with them is one that will work as well for a one-person office as it will for a big organization.

And speaking of organizations, one of the most delightful and insightful parts of the book makes it clear that zapping the gaps isn't dependent upon senior management support. It can be accomplished even under the most trying of circumstances.

If you think you've got troubles with a tough-minded, numbers-driven boss, wait until you meet Angela B. Krafft. In Angie, the authors have created the archetype bottom-line, results-oriented boss.

The problem the book's heroes, Bill and Sarah, have to solve is made more difficult because there simply isn't a bucket of money to throw on it. They have to rely on their own ingenuity—and some welcome support from a most unlikely source—to get things done. One very important message of this book is that correcting problems—zapping the gaps—is *your* responsibility. The lack of support, coaching, or money is no excuse not to perform yourself.

The strategy and system you'll discover to zap the gaps in your life are excellent, as is the message that it's your responsibility to do so, regardless of whether or not you work for an "Angie."

There is a third major message in *Zap the Gaps!* that comes with a delightful discovery at the end of the book which I'll not spoil by telling you of it here. But don't miss the message. Success isn't about knowing what to do. Success is about doing it! All of the knowledge in the world about gap zapping—even having perfect access to perfect mentors—doesn't account for squat unless you do something about it.

Ken Blanchard is famous both for his insight into management and organizational issues and for his ability to communicate solutions in ways others can grasp and put to work. I think it is safe to say that his writings have had a greater impact on the way successful organizations are actually run than those of any other person.

I have been fortunate and honored to have had the opportunity to sometimes assist Ken in his work. It is a particular pleasure to now welcome Dana and Jim Robinson into the circle of those privileged to be able to include the line "coauthor with Ken Blanchard" in their professional biographies.

—*Sheldon Bowles*

PREFACE

GAPS cost organizations billions every year. When people do not work at their best, everyone loses—the customer, the organization, the employee. No organization can ignore GAPS and still survive. This book is about identifying GAPS and their causes. It's about targeting those factors that cause GAPS and correcting them without jumping to solutions. The goal is to close GAPS in a systematic way so that ultimately there is a positive impact on all stakeholders.

The setting we chose for our story is that of a call center of a large computer hardware and software manufacturer/distributor. The operational results of a call center are largely dependent on human performance. Customer service representatives—or CSRs—are responsible for providing support to the customers who call in for help. The best CSRs are able to handle calls quickly and efficiently and resolve the customer's problem on the first call. But there are other CSRs who handle calls less efficiently, and the ensuing callbacks to revisit the problems can quickly jam the systems beyond capacity.

That is precisely the problem our main character faces in our story. But while the setting is his call center, the solutions that he discovers—and, more important, the process he goes through to discover them—are applicable to every organization of every size. Even a sole proprietorship with no other employees can benefit from the GAPS strategy.

On the surface, GAPS may appear to be a simple notion—a "pat formula" that can be grasped quickly as the reader flips through the pages of this book. In reality, though, it is a strategy that managers who seek continuing success for their organizations will have to apply on an ongoing basis. We think of GAPS as a sort of law that is nearly as rock-solid as the law of gravity. Sure, we can violate it, but we'd have to be somewhere in outer space to do so—and we might never return to earth.

GAPS should be unveiled in your workplace the moment you finish reading the last page of this book. You have nothing to lose and everything to gain by implementing these concepts immediately.

Not only will you gain, but so will your customers, organization, and employees.

Enjoy zapping those GAPS!

> —*Ken Blanchard*
> *Dana Robinson*
> *Jim Robinson*

ACKNOWLEDGMENTS

Ken would like to acknowledge the involvement and support of a number of people:

Dana Robinson and **Jim Robinson,** my coauthors, who have enhanced the viability and profitability of so many of their clients through the application of the GAPS strategy in areas of human performance. Their intensive work out in the trenches served as the inspiration for this book.

My wife, **Marjorie Blanchard,** who has lovingly identified some of my GAPS and has strengthened me as an individual as a result.

My son, **Scott,** my daughter, **Debbie,** her husband, **Humberto,** and my grandchildren, **Kurtis** and **Kyle,** who remind me that, as important as business is, loving relationships are the most important.

Steve Gottry, a friend and collaborative partner who lends his enthusiasm and creativity to a number of my projects.

Dottie Hamilt, whose amazing ability to juggle multiple projects and schedules (and keep on top of them all) helps me in immeasurable ways.

Margret McBride, my longtime literary agent whom I am pleased to call my friend, for her assistance in shepherding another concept into a published work.

Thanks to you all!

☙

*T*he Robinsons would like to add their word of thanks to the following people:

To **Ken Blanchard,** for pioneering the book genre known as "business fable" as a way of providing important ideas in a fun and easy-to-read manner, and for guiding us through the process of developing such a book.

To **Steve Gottry,** for creating characters and settings that bring our principles to life. This book represents one of the most remarkable examples of synergy in which we have been privileged to participate. From the first "kitchen table meeting" involving Ken, Steve, and the two of us, to the final manuscript, this has been a truly collaborative effort.

We appreciate our many **clients** from whom we continue to learn our gap-closing process. Our techniques have been sharpened through the work experiences we share, and it has been our privilege to collaborate with each and every one of them.

There are many people who have provided us with in-depth information regarding call centers and how they operate. In particular, we would like to acknowledge **Sheila Harrell, Shari Koonce,** and **Susan R. Schwartz.**

And without the support of our team of dedicated employees—**Karen Brewer, Lori Calhoun, Heather Rudar, Andrea Toth,** and **Linda Venturella**—we would not have been able to take time away from the office to work on this book. Their competence provided the confidence so necessary to allow us to devote our attention to this project.

Several individuals took time to review the manuscript and provide us with comments and feedback as to how it could be improved. They include: Erica Aranha, Pamela Benoit, Leslie Bussard, Paul Butler, Dale Cansler, Tammy Cansler, Richard Chang, Calla Crafts, Tamar Elkeles, Deidre Emery, Cindy L. Gage, Lael Good, Terri Hendricks, Christopher M. Iles, Kimberly Kleber, Bob Leininger, Sheila K. Loeffler, Lynn Marrable, Mary Morand, Holly Mortlock, Carman Nemecek, Jay W. Richey, Marilyn Richey, Linda Robinson, Jim Roderick, Lynn Rynbrandt, David Schwartz, Susan R. Schwartz, Nancy Scott, Janice Simmons, Lea M. Toppino, Kurt C. Treu, Craig Wilson, Mike Woerner, George Wolfe, and Deborah Zeilinger.

☙

There are several other behind-the-scenes individuals whose contributions deserve to be recognized:

Don Flavell, Golf Superintendent at Dobson Ranch and Riverview Golf Courses, Mesa, Arizona, for providing important background information on how golf courses are maintained and gaps are zapped.

We are indebted to the wonderful team at **William Morrow,** an imprint of HarperCollins Publishers. Our long-time friend, **Larry Hughes,** who is now retired, captured the vision for this project from its very conception. **Michael Morrison,** publisher at William Morrow, has provided continual support, as have **Joe Veltre,** a former senior editor who worked with Larry on the book in its early stages, and **Sarah Beam,** our always-cheerful and helpful editorial assistant. On the production side, **Kim Lewis,** managing editor, developed and oversaw the book's schedule; **Shannon Ceci,** production editor, coordinated the copyediting and proofreading; **Betty Lew,** design manager, created the interior design and **Richard Aquan,** senior art director, designed the cover. The marketing team is comprised of **Carrie Kania,** director of marketing, and **Libby Jordan,** vice president/associate publisher of William Morrow. **Kristen Green,** manager of publicity, serves as our capable publicist at William Morrow.

⊙

*P*resubmission production assistants/proofreaders, including: **Dave Gjerness, Linda Purdy, James Gottry,** and **Elisa Scinto.**

ZAP
THE
GAPS!

INTRODUCTION

*T*he man studied the trees with a puzzled expression on his face.

There were two of them—Mexican fan palms. He knew that they had been planted in that very spot on the same day. They were of exactly the same age, the same height and the same shape when they were transported from the nursery and placed in freshly dug holes in the desert soil.

Yet, as he looked at them, it was obvious that one had thrived while the other had somehow fallen behind. One was tall and sturdy in appearance; the other seemed dwarfed. The difference was striking.

"So what happened?" he asked. "They were planted at the same time. Why is one so much shorter? Why is there such a wide gap?"

"Good question" was the reply. "In order to answer it, we're going to have to get to the root causes."

"You mean it has something to do with the roots?" the man asked.

"I didn't exactly say that. There could be a number of considerations here. We can't just jump to solutions."

"I understand," said the man. But he really didn't. It was still a mystery to him.

With this brief glimpse into the future, we begin our story—the journey of William J. "Bill" Ambers, a man who is about to discover that trees and companies—and the people and teams who work for those companies—have a lot in common.

One
_____

THE ANNOUNCEMENT

This is not good news, Bill Ambers thought to himself as he scrolled through the announcement that had been delivered by E-mail to everyone in the company. *I'm sure it means nothing but trouble!*

It seemed that the company had just named a new division president of the Business Services Group—which is basically the call center for the large computer hardware and software manufacturer where Bill was employed as director of Customer Service. Bill quickly reflected on some of the more pertinent details about his new boss so that he could get a better picture of what might lie ahead. Many of his thoughts were merely speculation on his part, but he logged them in his mind anyway.

Angela B. Krafft. *Wonder if I'll have to call her
"Ms. Krafft" or if she goes by Angie?*

MBA from Stanford. *And me with four years at a
state university.*

Married. No children. *Probably no pets, either.
Very ordered life.*

With a competitor for the past eight years.
Wonder if she got canned?

Proven performer with a record of departmental
turnarounds. *Uh-oh!*

Bill hated getting new bosses. In his eleven years
with Dyad Technologies, he had endured three of
them. Ms. Krafft would be the fourth.

*They always come in and want to shake things up
right away,* he recalled. And terms such as "proven
performer" and "departmental turnarounds" were, in
Bill's opinion, clear cues that changes would abound
whether he liked it or not.

It took just two business days for Bill's fears to
become the potential nightmare he had predicted. He
got "the call."

"Ms. Krafft would like to see you tomorrow for
about half an hour. Do you have some time around ten
o'clock?" the scheduling administrator asked.

Bill paused for a moment as if to imply there was a crucial meeting on his schedule at ten. Of course, there wasn't. "I'm available," he replied as his blood pressure rose a bit.

"Good. President's office. Ten o'clock sharp. She's looking forward to meeting you."

Probably just a "get acquainted" meeting, Bill tried to assure himself. But he knew deep down that new bosses always spelled trouble. Why would this instance be any different?

☉

*B*ill actually wore a sport coat to work that day—despite the fact that he had dressed casually ever since the company relaxed its dress code. *Have to make a good first impression* was his driving motive.

Bill was normally a confident guy. He had enjoyed a number of successes in his nearly three decades in business. Since coming to Dyad, he had even been awarded the cherished "Eagle," the highest recognition offered by the company. It wasn't just the Divisional Eagle, either. It was the National Eagle. The Big Eagle.

But that was six years ago. Two bosses ago. Two major disappointments ago. The promotions he had anticipated never materialized. Two "strangers," both from outside Dyad's ranks, had moved into the vice presidencies he had sought. *I've worked hard, I'm dependable, why didn't I get those positions?*

Maybe this time it will be different, Bill thought as he went through the double glass doors and into the division president's waiting room at precisely 10:00 A.M. *Maybe this boss will make life better.*

"Mr. Ambers?" inquired a sophisticated-looking older woman whom Bill had never seen in his life.

"Yes."

"Ms. Krafft is expecting you. Go right in."

Bill Ambers opened the imposing door to the division president's office and was immediately taken aback. Gone were the stuffy vestiges of the past—the big mahogany desk, overblown leather chairs, and oil paintings of dead executives. In their place he saw a simple desk, an ergonomic chair, and a decorating style that could best be described as the "Tennis Hall of Fame": tennis rackets on display in Lucite cases and, as Bill would soon discover, autographed tennis balls arranged in a wooden box that had several shelves and a glass front. Pictures of all the tennis greats—both men and women—were personally autographed to "Angie" or "Angela."

The casually dressed division president rose from behind her desk, walked toward Bill, extended her hand, and greeted him warmly.

"Bill, I'm Angela Krafft. It's a pleasure to meet you. I've heard so much about you. Discovered you even won the National Eagle—'Big Bird,' I've heard it called."

Bill was immediately placed at ease. "That's right, Ms. Krafft. It was a real honor to win that award."

"Winning is always an honor, Bill. But please feel free to call me Angie. Formality has little place when we're all on the same team."

Bill again scanned the office. She was right. No formality here. Very comfortable. His eyes were once more drawn to the tennis paraphernalia. There were several trophies that he hadn't noticed previously. "You must have quite an interest in tennis," he offered.

"Yes. Actually, I love all sports. But tennis is my game. I played it in high school and college. I had hoped to turn pro, but when I bombed out in the Olympic tryouts, I settled on business."

She's refreshingly candid, Bill thought. Aloud he said, "That must have been a real disappointment."

"It was, but I've learned that a loss in one area of life doesn't mean I can't win in others. The win is very important to me. And that's why I surround myself with winners."

"I see," Bill said with a sudden burst of apprehension about where the conversation was headed.

"Bill, let me explain. I believe everyone in this company is a winner—or a potential winner. From what I've seen so far, Dyad does not hire junk."

"I see," Bill repeated. *Darn,* he thought. *I wish I had come up with a better response than that!*

"The problem at this call center is that our numbers are simply not in the win column. To borrow tennis terminology, we're even on sets, but we're down thirty-love in this game."

"What does that mean exactly?" an ashen-faced Bill asked.

"It means that I've reviewed the numbers from all three shifts of customer service representatives. Incoming calls are not being picked up as quickly as we want. One-call resolution is not even close to our goal. The abandonment rate is staggering."

Bill knew exactly what she was talking about. He knew that it often took five minutes or longer for callers to reach a real CSR. The target was two minutes or less. He knew that fewer than 70 percent of all problems were resolved in one call. And he knew that many callers abandoned their calls. They simply gave up—hung up.

Angie continued: "If we didn't offer our customers an integrated hardware/software solution here at Dyad, they would be fleeing us in droves, in favor of those companies that provide stellar customer service. And believe me, Bill, companies like that are out there. And the barriers to entry in our markets are not all that secure. We have to protect our market share. Our products are outstanding, but customer support has to match."

"What do you propose?" Bill asked, timidity evident in his voice.

"Bill, I need you to change the numbers. I need you to reverse the trends. We need to close the huge gaps in our performance. Frankly, Bill, I was brought in to turn the numbers around. My job—and yours, too—will be in jeopardy if we don't. I will support you in every way possible, but because you are the director of Customer Service, a lot of the responsibility falls on your shoulders. I'm looking for you to come up with the answers."

"I assure you that I'm doing the best I can," Bill sputtered. "But we have a number of problems that I can't solve. We have empty chairs. Not enough bodies. Our turnover rate is high, even for call centers. Training is not up to par. I don't think HR is doing its job."

"I have a question, Bill. I'd like to know if you view the HR staff as being true partners with your department? I know that in some companies they're viewed as simply gofers, but I believe the Human Resources Department can be your greatest ally. In today's business climate, we need to turn to one another, partner in every area, and depend on our associates to help us find solutions to meet our business needs. I want to let you in on a secret. I began my business career in HR. I later became a line manager—in a position very similar to yours. As a result, I can see both sides of the equation. I've learned that sometimes you have to dig for solutions. And sometimes the other guy has the shovel."

"I understand." These words were soon to become Bill's mantra. Whenever he didn't really understand, he responded with "I understand."

"Great!" the division president said with a smile. "I suggest that your course of action be to determine where the problems really are and then draft your best plan to solve them. You'll report back to me in two weeks, and we'll review your plan together."

Two weeks? That sure isn't much time! Bill thought as his new boss continued: "As you've probably guessed, I'm going to be meeting with every department head including, of course, Sarah Becker in HR. My philosophy is that we're not here to simply play the game and hope for a good outcome. We need to target our gaps and go for the win. All of us together." She stood up, walked around her desk, and extended her hand to a still-smarting Bill Ambers.

Bill shook her hand and headed toward the door. He couldn't wait to get out of there.

As he was turning the door handle, she stopped him.

"Bill, I read your personnel file. Your profile says you enjoy golf. Is that true?"

"It is!" He beamed as he recalled his hole in one on a 168-yard par three last April.

"I have a favor to ask then," Angela Krafft continued. "Our company supports a number of Phoenix charities, and one of them is the UMOM Homeless Shelter. I signed up to play in their benefit tournament, but I have a conflict that day. Would you be willing to pinch-hit for me? It's next Friday."

Bill could barely contain himself. He had heard all about this tournament. He could have a day off with pay, doing what he loved. And at one of the more exclusive country clubs in Scottsdale. "I'd be glad to!"

Bill walked back to his office with a broad grin on his face. *As new bosses go, she's not all that bad,* he thought to himself. But then, as the old saying goes, ignorance truly is bliss.

Two

ON THE GREENS

The day of the charity golf tournament couldn't arrive soon enough to suit Bill. He spent the intervening days wondering what he could do to increase performance among his CSRs. No apparent solution came immediately to mind.

Bright and early Friday morning Bill loaded his golf clubs into his trunk and headed for the course. *Beautiful day,* he thought to himself as he headed north on Scottsdale Road. *Hope my ball retriever is in my bag.* In his thirty-plus years of playing golf, Bill had launched more than his fair share of balls into every available water hazard. Despite his long straight drives, his "water-seeking" Titleists somehow even managed to land on the sprinkler heads in the middle of the fairways.

Bill took the first available parking space he could find, grabbed his bag, and headed for the already packed clubhouse.

"I'm here to play for Angela Krafft," he told the volunteer seated behind the "G to N" placard at the sign-in table.

The pleasant young woman scanned the players' list. "Ah, yes, here's her name. You'll be in Michael St. Vincent's foursome."

Michael St. Vincent . . . the name sounds familiar, Bill thought.

Bill grabbed a large cup of coffee on his way to the first tee. The other three members of his foursome— along with two golf carts—were already there.

"Anyone here named Michael St. Vincent?" Bill called out cheerily. "I'm part of his foursome."

"I'm Mike," said a brawny older man with a deep tan and chiseled features. "But you are definitely not Angela Krafft."

"No, I work for her. Name's Bill Ambers."

Mike extended his big hand. "Good to meet you, Bill. Actually, I was told that Angie wouldn't be able to join us. Glad she found someone to take her place."

"I'm glad she needed someone to fill in," Bill admitted with a grin.

"What's your handicap?" one of the other golfers asked.

"Twelve. On a good day."

Mike was impressed. "Looks like it's going to be a good round, boys."

Then to Bill he explained, "It's a scramble round. I can putt fairly well. Jerry here has an outstanding short game, and Ed's strength is his irons. So if you can get us off the tee, we could put together a winning game."

"It should be fun," Bill said. "Especially if we cheer each other on."

And fun it was. Bill had a great day off the tee— and he didn't hit a single water shot all day. Everyone contributed his part. They finished seventeen under par. That was good enough for second place.

Dinner was a time of celebration and enjoyable golf talk. But Bill wanted to know more about the guys in the foursome.

Two of them didn't seem to care about anything but golf, but one of them appeared to have an actual life outside the country club world. And that was Michael St. Vincent.

"What line of work are you in, Mike?" Bill asked during an uncomfortably long lull in the conversation.

"You might say I'm a gardener," Mike responded with a mischievous twinkle.

"I see," Bill said, wondering how a gardener could afford a membership at one of the top clubs in Scottsdale.

"Actually," Mike continued, "I started out in banking, but my love has always been things that grow—besides money. I started a landscaping business, then added several full-service nurseries and garden centers. You might have heard of my company—Saint's Nurseries and Landscaping."

"Heard of it? You're practically legendary!" Bill exclaimed. "When I built my new house, I checked around, and everyone recommended your company."

"I'm flattered."

"Seriously, I was totally blown away by your customer service. Your people checked back with me several times after the job was finished to make sure everything was doing well. They even fixed a couple of problems, no questions asked. They were so good that I decided to go with your service contract."

"I'm glad to hear that," Mike said, beaming. "I imagine you've seen my team hard at work on the grounds at your office, too. We've had the contract at Dyad Technologies for over three years. That's where you work, right?"

"That's the place. I'm the director of Customer Service for the call center."

"I'm afraid you'll have to explain to me what a call center is and does."

"It's pretty straightforward, really. Our company sells computers and software to a wide range of corporate users. Some of those companies are large enough to have information technology people on staff. But the smaller companies—and there are literally thousands of them—don't have the budget for IT support. Our call center technicians are available by phone to serve as their IT departments."

"So you solve problems for your customers?" Mike asked.

"Yes. We answer questions, eliminate software conflicts, help them determine if any internal parts have malfunctioned, and assist them with upgrades. Our systems are far more complex than typical desktop or laptop computers, so good customer service is important."

"How do you like working there?"

"Funny you should ask. I always thought I did a pretty good job. But we have this new boss—well, you obviously know her because I took her place in your foursome—and she's really taking a close look at everything. I know I have to improve our numbers or I'm history, but I hardly know where to begin."

"You open to some advice from an old gardener?" Mike asked sympathetically.

"I'm open to all the help I can get," Bill admitted.

"When I have a problem to solve, I always start by asking the question, 'What are the needs?' "

"That's easy. I *need* to make my numbers. Gotta make my boss happy, you know."

Mike laughed. "Okay, that's a start. But let me show you what I mean."

He took out a pen, grabbed a slightly soggy cocktail napkin and drew a rectangle. Within that rectangle, near the top, he wrote the words "Business Needs."

"The first thing you have to know is what the business needs are of your operation. What is your reason for existing?"

"That's easy to answer, too," Bill replied. "Our reason for being is to provide customer support for the people and companies who buy our hardware and software."

"That's it?"

"Well, there's more to it than that. The new boss told me that we're not here to simply play the customer service game. We have to go for the win, as she calls it, and provide stellar customer service so that we don't lose market share."

"How do you know if you're providing 'stellar customer service,' as you put it?"

Bill thought for a moment. "I guess if we're meeting or exceeding our operational metrics, then we're doing our job."

"Metrics? Can you explain that to me?"

"Sure. Let's say the goal is to have our customers' calls answered by a live CSR in two minutes or less, but it actually takes five minutes on average. And let's say that our goal is to resolve the customers' problems on their first call to our center eighty-five percent of the time, but we succeed only seventy percent of the time. In those two instances, among many, we're failing to meet our metrics—the standards that we're committed to achieving."

Mike's expression was thoughtful. "Okay, that explains things from your company's perspective. But how do you know how the customers feel about this? Maybe they don't care if it takes you five minutes to answer their calls."

"Oh, but they do. There's another metric called the 'abandonment rate.' That's a measure of those callers who give up and hang up without ever talking to a CSR. Long waits obviously contribute to high abandonment rates."

"I understand that, too. But how do you know if those callers who do get through are satisfied customers?"

Two answers came to Bill's mind. "First, we have our managers hook up a second headset and listen in on many of the calls. They can pretty much tell how satisfied the customers are by their comments and the tone of their voices. Second, an independent company sends E-mail surveys to several of our customers on an ongoing basis to get their feedback."

"That makes sense to me," Mike agreed. "I'm well aware that in my business there are scores of competitors who would love to capture my customers. That's why we work so hard on customer service. You mentioned that my team continued to call you back to make sure you were happy and everything was growing as it should. That's part of what we do to create raving fans. You bought into it, too, which is why you opted for our service contract. Now let me show you something else."

Mike drew another rectangle inside the first and wrote the words "Performance Needs" within the new box, again near the top.

"What I'm trying to demonstrate here is that *business needs* drive *performance needs*. In other words, what do your CSRs need to do more, better, or differently to help you meet your business needs?"

"Good question," Bill replied, "but I'm not sure I know the answer. Maybe our CSRs need to chitchat less so the calls can end quicker and they can get on to the next one, but that doesn't fit with our goal of offering friendly customer service. I know they have to resolve problems on the first call because that eliminates callbacks, which frees up more phone lines."

"Do you have any thoughts on how CSRs can actually achieve the desired results, especially when some of the goals seem to be at odds with one another?"

"Nothing fresh and revolutionary pops into my mind," Bill confessed. "We probably need more training to make certain that our people do a better job."

"Possibly. But don't go jumping to solutions," Mike cautioned. "Training may not be the answer. You may need to look deeper than that. Let me show you the next component."

"Another box, right?"

Mike laughed. "Right." He drew a smaller box within the second box and wrote these words inside its borders: "Work Environment and Capability Needs."

BUSINESS NEEDS

PERFORMANCE NEEDS

WORK ENVIRONMENT AND CAPABILITY NEEDS.

"I think I know where you're going with this, but I'm still not exactly sure how it all fits together," Bill said thoughtfully.

"Fortunately, I have a better way to explain it. Do you have plans for tomorrow afternoon?" Mike asked.

Bill groaned. "Only if you call wallpapering the kitchen a plan."

"Can you put it off until next week?"

"It's a tough choice. But sure, why not? What do you have in mind?"

"Golf, of course. Right here. I booked a 1 P.M. tee time with Jerry, but he can't make it."

"Sounds good," Bill confirmed. "See you then."

Three
_____

LESSONS FROM GRASS

We're really here for two reasons," Mike said as he prepared to tee off on that warm and sunny Saturday afternoon. "First and foremost, of course, is to play golf. The second is to learn about grass."

"Did I hear you right? Grass?" Bill asked.

"That's right," Mike replied as he lined up his driver behind the ball. He drew the club head back slowly, took his best swing, and heard a disconcerting "whack!"

"Drive for show, putt for dough," Mike muttered under his breath as his ball sliced into the rough.

Bill laughed despite himself. "So you're going to teach me about *tall* grass, apparently."

"Very funny," Mike responded grudgingly.

Bill teed off, and, sure enough, the ball sailed straight and true and ended up in the middle of the fairway—dangerously close to a pool of standing water—almost 260 yards away.

"Okay, I can see I have my work cut out for me," Mike observed. "I don't suppose you want to make this a bit more interesting?"

Bill took his host up on his offer of a friendly bet, and play became more intense—with a few dollars riding on the match.

They finished the first nine, and Mike drove the cart toward the tenth tee. "Let's take a break and talk for a few minutes before we play the back nine."

"Okay. What's the subject of the conversation?" Bill was curious about what could be so important that it would interrupt play.

"Look around you," Mike suggested. "What do you see?"

"I see mountains and sky and other golfers and the clubhouse."

"No, no. Not all that. I'm talking about the grass. What do you see?"

"Okay, I see grass," Bill said, remembering that Mike had said one of the reasons they were playing was to learn about grass.

"Yes, but what do you notice about the grass?"

"Well, I see the grass on the fairway, the longer grass in the rough, and the short grass on the green and on the tee."

"Exactly!" Mike said triumphantly. "And they're not all the same grass. Different types of grasses are used for different purposes. Remember the illustration I drew last night?"

"Yes. As a matter of fact, I saved it."

"The outer box was 'Business Needs,' right?"

"Right."

"What do you suppose are the business needs of this golf course?"

"To attract members so they can collect dues, make money, and stay in business," Bill ventured.

"That's basically it. And what do you suppose the people who manage this course would have to do more, better, or differently to compete effectively with the many other golf courses in the Phoenix area?"

"I don't really know. Maybe they'd have to charge lower initiation fees or lower monthly or annual dues."

Mike laughed. "I wish that were the case, but the fact is, this club has the highest fees of any course in Arizona."

"What is it then?" Bill wondered aloud.

"My feeling is that among the ways they build their edge and meet their objectives are by maintaining a championship-level course, providing clean and comfortable facilities for members' events, and offering outstanding food. And, of course, competent, friendly, and helpful employees are an absolute necessity. These are largely employee performance matters."

"Makes sense to me," Bill agreed.

"What would you imagine the food staff, for example, needs to do more, better, or differently to ensure the club's success?"

"I can think of a few things," Bill said as he reflected on some of his favorite restaurants. "Reservations are honored promptly, the wait staff is friendly and they smile when they take the order, food is served hot, special requests are met cheerfully, and most important—the bill is correct!"

Mike chuckled. "Good! Good! All excellent thoughts. And, as a matter of fact, you've just described the dining experience here exactly."

"I did notice that the banquet meal was very well prepared and efficiently served," Bill said, recalling the previous evening.

"Naturally, the club does regular surveys and encourages members to turn in comment cards, too. Even the smallest concerns are addressed immediately. I could, for example, report a large divot on the second fairway to a ranger, and it would be repaired almost immediately."

"Amazing! So that would fall under the category of 'maintain a championship-level golf course.' They must really work hard to keep it up."

"That's part of it, for certain," Mike agreed. "The grounds people are not only doing more, but they're doing it better and they're doing it differently. Of course, the other part of what makes this a top championship course is the grass."

"Oh, come on, Mike," Bill chided. "Grass is just grass. Sure, you have short grass on the green and longer grass on the fairways, but other than that . . ."

"There's major science, technology, and specialized skill behind great golf courses, Bill, and it relates to the third 'needs' box I drew for you."

Bill was puzzled.

"We've already discussed the fact that among the things that help a country club meet its business needs are excellent food service and a championship-level course, right?"

"Right."

"And we've discussed that the performance of the people who prepare good, hot food and serve it in a friendly, prompt manner is important."

"Right."

"The next step, then, is to make certain that capability needs can be met. In this category, the skills and knowledge of the individual are key. The chefs can't prepare properly seasoned dishes if they don't know the difference between oregano and salt. The wait staff can't provide good service if they don't know how to open a bottle of fine wine or keep track of their tables so that the guests get what they have ordered. It's the same thing when it comes to eighteen holes of good golf. A qualified superintendent and competent grounds people must have the skills to watch over every detail, anticipate potential problems, and remedy actual ones.

"Finally, work environment needs must be considered. The chefs can't prepare hot food if the ovens don't work. The wait staff can't serve wine if there are no corkscrews on the premises. And in terms of the golf course, the minimum work environment requirements are good irrigation systems, quality tools such as fairway and greens mowing equipment, and . . . the right grass for every application."

"You're telling me grass is not just grass then," Bill suggested.

"Exactly. To be specific, each type of grass used must be capable of meeting the expectations of golfers. On greens you'll generally find bent grass. It has high shoot density, which means there are more blades per square inch than found in other grasses. It has a very fine leaf blade and can be mowed to heights of about one-tenth to one-eighth of an inch. That results in a smooth, even surface—exactly what's needed for putting."

"How about the fairways?" asked Bill.

"That's a different story. Generally, in this climate, we use Tifway, a type of Bermuda grass. It stands up well under the traffic of carts and golfers, and the groundskeepers find it easier to repair divots on Tifway as well. It also has a high shoot density but is mowed only to a height of five-sixteenths to three-eighths of an inch. The rough areas are usually the same grass but are maintained at a greater height."

"I think I understand. The performance needs determine both the work environment needs and the capability needs. In order for the groundskeepers to provide a championship golf course, they need the right grass, the right tools to cut the grass, and the right systems to irrigate the grass. So these things are their work environment needs."

"Exactly! But, Bill, there are other 'concealed' work environment considerations, too. They're invisible to the golfer but are of utmost importance."

Bill replied with nothing more than a puzzled expression, so Mike tried to explain in layman's terms. "The grounds people can't simply scatter seed, water it, mow it, and hope to have a championship golf course as a result. The environment has to be right. In most instances, the environment is composed of things the golfer never sees. They are under the surface. For example, before the greens are planted, there's a lot of sub-surface preparation. On this course the soil beneath the green is about eighty-five percent sand and fifteen percent organic matter. The sand is tested in labs for precise particle size so that, say, ten years down the road, proper drainage is still provided. This all creates the necessary environment for a championship-grade golf course."

"I had no idea it's such an exact science!"

"More so than you could imagine. There are ongoing work environment considerations, too. The shorter grass on the greens and on the tee boxes has to be nourished with higher amounts of nitrogen, phosphorous, and potassium than the longer grass on the fairways. The wrong balance of nutrients could result in burned-out grass. Watering and drainage are vital considerations, too."

Bill was impressed. "It all sounds very complex. How do they find the qualified people they need?"

"Have you ever heard of accredited turf programs?"

"Can't say that I have."

"Because there's so much science and technology behind golf courses, superintendents generally attend turf programs. Universities such as Michigan State, Penn State, and the University of Arizona, among others, have long-established programs that offer two- or four-year degrees in the specialized curriculum of turf grass science. It's a demanding field of study, and country clubs like ours compete to attract the top graduates. The business needs of this country club— including the need to achieve our membership and revenue goals—are supported by the performance of the superintendent and the groundskeepers. Their performance, in turn, is supported by their own capabilities as well as by the tools, equipment, and other resources that are part of the work environment."

"Amazing! I'm impressed. And I'm beginning to see how this fits together. The needs are all interrelated, which is why you drew boxes inside of boxes." Bill took out the wrinkled cocktail napkin and studied it carefully.

"You've got it!" Mike applauded. "The thing is, it's a similar situation in any company. To get the results you want, you first have to understand the business needs. Then you have to determine the performance requirements of people to meet those needs. To ensure performance you have to make certain that people are truly capable and that their work environment needs are being met. If any piece isn't in place, you're going to have problems. I can guarantee it."

Bill was impressed. "I have to admit that's the most useful information I've ever picked up on a golf course."

"Great! Glad to hear it."

"Now," Bill offered, "let me make a couple of suggestions on your grip and stance to help you straighten out your drives."

"You saying my performance isn't what it should be?" Mike joked.

"Looks like it to me. You need to improve your capabilities. And I'm here to help!"

Four
_____

"SHOULD" IS GOOD

Bill never did get to the kitchen wallpaper that weekend. But when he told his wife about the things he had learned on the golf course, she didn't seem to mind at all. "I could have used some of that information a couple of weeks ago myself," she said wistfully.

Monday mornings usually didn't hold much favor with Bill, because they marked the beginning of a new reporting period—along with the end of the last period. That meant every problem that had cropped up during the previous week would be called to his attention. The report hardly ever brought good news.

This particular Monday, however, was different. There was a decided bounce in Bill's step. He was ready to take on every challenge. *Go get 'em, Tiger!* he thought to himself—in thoroughly non-Bill jargon.

Bill knew that his task for the next few weeks was
to make Division President Angela Krafft a happy
boss. All he had to do was align performance needs
with business needs. And to accomplish that, all he
had to do was make sure that capability and work
environment needs were met. He had to figure out
what his people needed to do "more, better, or
differently" and then get them to do it. The word
"training" kept popping into his mind.

This sounds like a job for HR! he thought with
tremendous confidence.

When Bill got to his desk, he scanned the
employee directory for his counterpart in HR. *Ah,
here it is! Sarah Jane Becker, Human Resources
Manager.* He dialed Sarah's extension. He was greeted
by her voice mail response and left a brief message.

"Hi, Sarah, this is Bill Ambers at 2350. Could you
please give me a call? I need your help ASAP.
Thanks!"

Bill went about his morning tasks, including his
ritual review of the dismal activity report from the
previous week. At about 10:30, the phone rang.

"Hi, Bill, this is Sarah."

"Hi, Sarah."

"Sorry I'm so late in getting back to you. I had a
meeting with the new president."

"I understand completely. I've had one of those myself."

"What can I do for you, Bill?"

"Do you have time for a quick meeting? I have some problems to solve, and I could use your help."

"Sure. I'll be free in about twenty minutes. Your place or mine?"

"How about the cafeteria at eleven o'clock?"

"Eleven it is."

☉

*B*ill showed up at the cafeteria at 10:58, by his watch. Sarah was already there, sipping on a machine-made mocha.

"Thanks for meeting on such short notice, Sarah."

"No problem. What's the scoop?"

"The scoop is that our numbers are not what they should be. First-call resolution needs improvement, response time is not all that hot—well, you know the usual problems. You see the reports."

"Yes, I know. And I've been thinking about what I could do to help."

"As I see it, we have two distinct problems. We solve them, and all the numbers will get into line."

Sarah leaned forward. "I'm listening."

"Okay, great!" Bill began. "The first problem is turnover. My guess is that every call center has the same problem. The job is high stress with low pay. I mean, I wouldn't want to do phone time myself. So we need to hire people on a fast track. Fill those empty chairs with warm bodies."

Sarah made notes, looked up, smiled, and said, "Uh-huh."

"The other thing," Bill continued, "is that we need to provide more training. Some of these new hires barely know how to say 'How may I help you?' let alone actually provide any meaningful help."

"Uh-huh."

"A strict, well-designed program—maybe using some outside consultants—would be just the trick."

"Uh-huh."

"Then we could develop a testing regimen to make sure that the trainees have assimilated the information and can apply it appropriately."

"Uh-huh."

"Sarah, you keep saying uh-huh. What are you *really* saying?"

"Bill, this all sounds great—"

"Uh-huh."

"—except for one thing."

"Which is?"

"My meeting with Angela Krafft this morning. I asked for a budget increase. She said no. She cautioned me that I have to demonstrate how HR actually adds value to the company. She wants to know what we really do to help close the obvious performance gaps around here. The bottom line is that she told me I have to find creative ways to go for the win."

" 'Go for the win,' she says. 'Close the gaps and go for the win.' How are we supposed to close gaps and go for the win when our hands are tied? It's like—it's like playing tennis with our rackets strapped behind our backs!" Bill sputtered.

"That *is* the problem, isn't it?" Sarah asked rhetorically.

Bill was silent as he pondered this most adverse situation. Then a smile slowly brightened his face. "There's someone I want you to meet!"

"Who's that?"

"You'll see," Bill said as he whipped out his cell phone and dialed a number scrawled on a scrap of paper he had been carrying around in his pocket. "Michael St. Vincent, please." The line was silent for a few seconds.

"Mike here. What can I do to help make your life perfect?"

Oddest greeting I've ever heard, Bill thought. "Mike, this is Bill Ambers. You know—long drives, lousy putts."

"Sure, Bill. What can I do for you?"

"Do you have time for lunch today?"

"Well, I was supposed to fly out to D.C. on Air Force One, but I guess I can reschedule. What's up?"

Funny, Bill thought. "I'd love to buy you lunch," he said.

"Sounds good. But I'll buy. That'll make me feel a little better about taking your money last Saturday."

"Great! The truth is, I'd forgotten all about it."

"Monday is usually my day for Italian. You okay with that?"

"Italian it is. I'd like our HR manager to join us if you don't mind."

"Fine with me. Twelve-thirty at Brunello's? You know where that is?"

"Sure do. See you there."

☻

W hat's on your mind?" Mike asked as he was about to dig into his hearts of palm and artichoke salad.

"I went back to work this morning all excited about the things I learned from you—about business needs and performance needs and capability needs and work environment needs."

"And . . . ?"

"I decided that the two things we had to do to get those things in alignment were to make sure that every chair was filled by a warm body, and then make sure those people were thoroughly trained and tested."

Mike thought about this for a moment, then turned to Sarah. "What were your thoughts on this?"

"I agreed, but it doesn't much matter. I had a meeting with our new division president to ask for a budget increase, and she turned me down."

Mike grinned. "That must be the infamous Angela Krafft, huh?"

"One and the same."

"Here's where you're getting this all wrong," Mike suggested. "Before you can throw potential solutions at a problem, you have to do one important thing."

"What?" Bill and Sarah asked in unison.

"You have to *go for the 'shoulds.'* "

"Huh?" they again asked in unison.

"Go for the 'Shoulds,' " Mike repeated as he reached into his shirt pocket and pulled out a small stack of cards. Some were blue, some yellow, some green, some red, some purple. He plucked two yellow cards from the stack. "I carry this card with me practically all the time. I have a well-worn copy in my wallet. It serves as a constant reminder of a simple principle that has guided my business for many years."

He handed a copy of the card to each of them, and they studied it as if it were written in some indecipherable code.

"More, better, or differently" always

equals the "should be."

Go for the "shoulds"!

"Okay, Mike," Bill ventured. "I have no idea what this means."

"I know, but I'm not telling!" Sarah said with a feisty grin.

Mike laughed heartily and continued. "You need to determine what the 'shoulds' are. The 'shoulds' need to be your number-one focus, and you have to go for them. In your case, you have two kinds of 'shoulds.' The first ones are what I heard you call metrics. You want quick response to incoming calls? That's a 'should be.' Go for it! You want improved first-call resolution of customers' problems? Another 'should be.' Go for it! You want a lower call abandonment rate? Go for it! Those are your operational 'shoulds.' Go for the 'shoulds'!"

Bill was getting frustrated. "Okay, we basically know what the 'shoulds' are. Two minutes, eighty-five percent, and—"

Mike interrupted. "Yes, that's one set of 'shoulds.' But I mentioned that there are two kinds. The second kind are the performance 'shoulds.' It all goes back to what your CSRs need to do more, better, or differently. The 'shoulds' represent the desired behaviors."

"There has to be a next step, right?" Sarah asked.

"Yes. And there is. You need to identify which of your CSRs are the star performers, and you need to find out what they do more, better, or differently."

"I understand," Bill responded without much conviction.

Mike was not convinced. "This is really important, Bill! How do you know who your top CSRs are?"

"We know because of our shift managers. As I mentioned the other day, they wander around the room and plug their headsets into the CSRs' consoles. They listen in on the calls and help with problems as needed. The CSRs with fewer problems are the better performers."

"Are you sure?" Mike asked.

"Well . . . yes. Their operational results demonstrate it. They resolve more problems on the first call than other CSRs do. And the average duration of their conversations is shorter so they can handle more calls."

"Which is more important? Solving the problem on the first call or keeping the call short?"

"It doesn't really matter, because the boss says we have to improve all the metrics."

"I see," said Mike.

Sarah jumped in. "Let's say that we can identify all of our top performers. What do we do next?"

"You have to ask questions. Ask your stars if they know what they do to achieve the results they're getting. Find out their secrets."

"And you think that will really work?"

"I sure do! Here's an example. A few years ago I decided to offer a whole slew of high-quality gas-powered garden tools in my stores. I mean, I had it all: leaf blowers, chain saws, riding lawn mowers, hedge trimmers. They were higher priced than the competition but worth the extra money. Anyway, they bombed like crazy. Sales were underwhelming. So I was stuck with a ton of inventory. I had to carry the interest and use up valuable floor space. I had a real business need. 'What am I going to do?' I wondered."

"What did you do?"

"Nothing, actually. Not at first, anyway. Then something happened that I hadn't expected. One of my showroom employees quit, so I ran an ad and hired a replacement. I thought I'd still have the same problem with the unsold inventory, but I was wrong."

Bill and Sarah both leaned forward in their chairs as if to say, "Tell us more."

"Within a week of hiring this new guy, I noticed that some of the merchandise was beginning to sell. I had no clue what was going on. Within three weeks he came to my office and informed me that we had to reorder some of the mowers, trimmers, and leaf blowers, along with a couple of gas-powered wood chippers. I was floored! I asked him, 'How is it that everyone has been selling so much of this stuff all of a sudden?' "

"What did he say?"

"He said, 'Actually, I sold it all myself.' I couldn't believe it. I asked him what his secret was."

"And . . . ?"

"He said, 'I figured our greatest competition was from the discount stores. So when customers came in to buy plants or fertilizer, I asked them if they had seen our line of powered lawn tools. They told me that they already had a lawn mower—or whatever—and I asked them how old it was, if they were happy with it, and when they planned to replace it. Then I told them why our products were so much better than the tools they could get from other sources. I showed them features that the other tools didn't have and told them the specific benefits of those features. I also pointed out that we offer service after the sale—something the discounters can't do.' "

"That's it?" Bill asked.

"That's it."

"Did you order more of the tools?" Sarah wondered.

"Sure did. But that's not the end of the story. Once I uncovered the performance 'shoulds'—what my star performer was doing that the others weren't— I passed that information along to them so they could achieve similar results."

"Did it work?"

"Like a charm! I'm now the largest combined dealer for those products west of the Mississippi."

"So you're saying we should do something like that?"

"Bingo!"

Sarah protested: "We've been told there's no new money in our budgets. This sounds like an expensive proposition. We can't afford to add a new program."

Mike was amused. "Could you afford to have lunch with me today?"

"Of course. It was our lunch break. Free time, you know?"

"So tomorrow start taking your star employees to lunch. Get them to tell you their secrets, one-on-one. That won't cost your company very much at all."

"That doesn't sound like a very formal, professional approach, though," Bill argued.

Mike smiled. "You're not researching a doctoral thesis here. You're not mining scientific data. You're not trying to come to some kind of consensus. You're simply seeking to solve a problem. You need to go for the 'shoulds.' That's what going for the win is all about, in my opinion."

If I hear "going for the win" one more time, I think I'm going to lose my lunch, Bill thought. Aloud he said, "What you're saying is that we simply have to go out there and ask a lot of questions."

"Not exactly. Anyone can ask questions. What you have to do is ask the right questions right."

"What do you mean by that?"

"Good question. But first let me ask you a few questions. Do you like your job, Bill?"

"Basically, yes."

"Do you think that Dyad is a good company to work for?"

"Sure. Yes."

"Do you believe that there could be better customer service departments at other companies?"

With that question Bill got a bit defensive. "Hard to tell. I don't know. I guess. Yeah, probably."

"Sarah, do you know what was wrong with all of the questions I asked Bill?"

"I sure do," Sarah responded. "They were all closed questions. They weren't what I've heard described as high-yield questions. The only answers they drew out were things like yes, no, and maybe."

"Precisely!" Mike lauded. "I extracted answers from Bill, but I didn't obtain any useful information. I asked questions, but I didn't ask the right questions right. Now let me try again, asking open-ended questions."

"Fine."

"Bill, what things do you like about your job, and what things do you believe need improvement?"

"Okay, I see what you mean," Bill said. "But to obtain usable data, don't I have to ask questions that lead to answers that can be quantified and categorized?"

"In some cases, that's true," Mike agreed. "But in your case, quantification has little value. You're looking for the performance 'should be.' You need to dig for the answers, and your star performers are the best source of those answers. In the case of my sales guy who sold all the lawn equipment, I had to ask him what he was doing more, better, or differently. It was only when I got those answers that I could help my other salespeople discover how to achieve similar results."

Sarah glanced at her watch. "Oh, my! Bill, I'm due at a meeting that was supposed to start almost ten minutes ago!"

Sarah and Bill stood up to leave. "I'm sorry I made you late," Mike said. "I shouldn't have spent so much time talking about 'shoulds.' "

"That's okay," Sarah said graciously. "This has been extremely helpful."

"It sure has," Bill added. "Thanks for your time . . . and thanks for lunch."

And off they went, eager to change their world.

Five

_____

GO, NO GO

*B*ill and Sarah approached the task before them with major enthusiasm. They were sure that once they identified the "should be" behaviors of their top CSRs, they could implement a program to transfer all those desired practices to the rest of the team.

"This will be the most effective training program we've ever had!" Bill suggested.

"You could be right," Sarah agreed. "Once we ask our top people what their secrets are, it should be fairly easy to codify them into a training program. This could revolutionize the training process for CSRs worldwide!"

"One minor problem, though," Bill conceded. "I have two kids in college and a high schooler who eats more food than an entire NFL football team. I don't really have the money to buy a lot of lunches."

"On top of that, you know we can't just ask our hourly employees to volunteer their time," Sarah reminded him. "The law says we have to pay them. Let's at least try to talk Angie into covering those costs."

Sarah and Bill managed to get on Angie's calendar first thing the next morning. So punctual were the three of them that they practically crashed into one another in front of Angie's door.

"Thank you for seeing us on such short notice," Sarah said as she shook Angie's hand and quickly took a seat.

"Yes, we really appreciate it," Bill added.

"Never a problem," the division president said. "I see 'being available' as one of my key job responsibilities."

Refreshing change, Bill thought as he recalled the closed-door policy of Angie's predecessor.

"We've been working together to solve the customer service–related problems we've been experiencing," Bill began. "I know you asked me to submit a written plan next week, but we're hot on the trail of something, so we wanted to get together with you right away. We believe we can solve the problem of gaps in our CSR performance by discovering what our top performers do well and then transferring those skills to the typical CSRs."

Angie thought for a moment. "That's an interesting idea, Bill. How do you propose to accomplish this?"

"We'd like to take our best CSRs to lunch, one-on-one."

"You mean *two*-on-one," Sarah interjected.

"That's right. I'm sorry. Two-on-one. Obviously, Sarah would be directly involved in the process."

Angie was ready with her response. "Have you calculated what this will cost in terms of overtime pay and providing the meals?"

"We believe that if we interview eight people, or about five percent of our CSRs, for one hour each, we can accomplish our objectives," Sarah responded. "That should cost no more than six hundred dollars."

"Obviously, you're not taking them to a five-star restaurant," Angie said with a smile. "I realize that's not a lot of money, but little things do add up. I'm wondering if there's not another way to achieve the same goal—one that won't cost any money at all."

Man, is she cheap! Bill thought to himself.

"Do you have a specific thought on that?" asked Sarah.

"As a matter of fact, I do. I suggest that you do more of what you already do. Plug into the consoles of your top performers and listen to how they interact with customers. See if you can detect any patterns."

"The shift managers and I have listened a lot in recent months," Bill protested, "and we haven't noticed any patterns."

Angie's response was terse. "Perhaps you need to do a better job of listening."

Sarah immediately came to Bill's rescue. "The reason we're suggesting the two-on-ones, Angie, is that we believe we can solve the problem more quickly than if we were to simply listen in without being able to ask high-yield questions. And we are under the impression that the numbers have to change as soon as possible."

Angie carefully considered Sarah's argument. "You do raise a good point—two of them. I'm going to sign off on your proposal. Six hundred dollars certainly isn't going to break us."

☉

*B*ill and Sarah left Angie's office with smiles on their faces. When they had rounded the corner 40 feet down the corridor, they gave each other an elated high five.

They couldn't wait to get started. "Let's talk to some of our star CSRs tomorrow," one of them suggested. And so they did.

Much to their surprise, the top performers they contacted were eager to share their thoughts in the two-on-one lunch meetings. In less than two weeks, Bill and Sarah had conducted all their interviews and had compiled a concise report of their findings. The following Monday morning they showed up at Angie's door armed with copies of their report.

Angie was pleased to see them. "I'm glad you took this task so seriously. What did you discover?"

Bill jumped in immediately. "Amazingly, we uncovered twelve distinct behaviors that we believe set our top performers apart from our more typical CSRs. You'll find them listed on page two, with detailed explanations on pages three and four. Our plan for the future follows on pages five and six."

Angie turned to page two and studied the summary.

Dyad's Top-Performing CSRs

• Ask open-ended, high-yield questions to gather information about the customer's problem.

• Listen well and acknowledge the problem.

• Adjust to the customer's responses based on his or her emotions or feelings.

- Are not argumentative and are not likely to be offensive or defensive in tone.

- Use the customer's name frequently during the conversation.

- Seek out what the customer expects from the company and clearly specify the actions the company will take.

- Offer a realistic time frame in which the problem will be solved.

- Exhibit patience and allow the customer to vent.

- Are able to perform multiple tasks simultaneously without disrupting the flow of the call.

- Redirect the conversation to get back on track, which helps reduce the overall length of the call.

- Apologize for any CSR or company errors.

- Thank the customer for the call and seek information on the customer's degree of satisfaction with the outcome.

Angie put the report down on her desk and said, "This seems quite thorough to me. Good work!"

"Thank you," Bill responded.

Sarah added her thoughts: "One obvious trait that was not included in this report was that of 'outstanding product knowledge,' although our best CSRs clearly have thorough product knowledge. We focused more on behaviors. You might call them the specific practices exhibited by our most effective CSRs."

"I see," Angie acknowledged. "What do you plan to do with this information?"

Sarah answered, "If you turn to page five, you'll see that our solution is to provide training in these practices to our more typical CSRs so that they, too, can join the ranks of the top performers. We've outlined the program and the proposed budget, along with the expected outcome."

Bill and Sarah sat in silence as Angie studied the proposal. Moments later she put the report down. "I'm afraid I can't go along with your plan," she announced firmly.

"Why?" demanded Bill, his blood pressure rising. "Is it the money?"

"No, it's not the money."

I think she wants me to fail just so she can bring in some college classmate to replace me, Bill thought. *Anyone with half a brain can see that this is a good plan. No, it's a* great *plan! She's turning out to be the nightmare boss I thought she'd be.*

"What is it then?" Sarah queried.

"It's very simple. You state in this report that you want to provide uniform training to every CSR. I have several concerns about that. First, we don't have an adequate number of CSRs to allow us to pull more than two or three of them off-line at any given time. Second, because of that fact, the training process will take too long. Third, it will be very costly. And finally—and this is the big one—how do you know that most of our CSRs lack the specific skills you've outlined or that training will make a difference?"

Bill and Sarah both hesitated.

"How do you know that the lack of certain skills is the only reason some CSRs don't perform as well as others?"

"Um . . . we . . . uh . . . we don't," they admitted.

"I can't imagine any of our CSRs being so out of touch with good business practices that they wouldn't use the customer's name during the call. But how do you know that's even an issue with the customer?"

"We don't."

"If you were to choose only six of the items on your list to target for training, how would you know which six to include?"

"We . . . we wouldn't know."

"I suggest that until you can answer those questions, you don't even think about building a new training program. You need to make sure you focus on those practices that truly impact effectiveness."

She is one tough cookie, Bill thought as he rose to his feet. *I guess she told us!*

Sarah and Bill both shook Angie's hand as warmly as they could under the circumstances and then headed back to their respective offices.

"I'll call you in a few minutes," Bill whispered as they parted company.

☺

*B*ill sat silently behind his desk for a few minutes, trying to erase the sting of his encounter with Angie. When he had recovered sufficiently, he dialed Sarah's extension.

"That was brutal" were his first words when she answered her phone.

"Sure was. I feel like a college freshman who was sent to the dean's office for blowing up the chemistry lab."

"If you're trying to cheer me up with humor, forget it. I can't be cheered after I've been jeered."

"All right, here's another idea. Four letters: M-I-K-E."

Six

THE "IS" IS WHERE THE GAP IS

You two look like a couple of kids whose puppy ran away from home," Mike said as he welcomed Sarah and Bill into his office.

"Thanks a lot. Truth is, I think we both feel about that bad."

"What happened?"

"We did exactly what you suggested," Bill explained. "We interviewed our top performers and identified twelve key behaviors that we believe make them successful."

"Okay. Then what?"

"We scheduled a meeting with our boss and presented our findings."

"Then what?"

"We outlined our proposal for a new training program to teach these behaviors to the rest of the CSRs."

"How did she respond to that?"

"Not well. She told us that unless we could make a case that the skills lacking in some of our CSRs are actually impacting performance, training is out of the question."

Mike contemplated this for a moment. "I think I see the problem here. You not only have to go for the 'shoulds.' You have to *analyze the 'is.'*"

"Analyze the 'is'? You've really lost me here," Bill admitted.

"Me, too," Sarah chimed in.

"That's why we're here, folks," Mike said confidently. "I'm going to walk you through this, and then it's up to you to apply it."

"Fair enough," they both agreed.

Mike dug into his shirt pocket, found two red cards, and handed one each to Sarah and Bill. They read:

Everything we are currently doing

equals the "is."

The "is" is where the gap is!

Analyze the "is"!

Sarah and Bill studied the cards in silence. Mike didn't even wait for them to respond. "We've already discussed what the 'shoulds' should look like at your call center, both in terms of the operational 'shoulds' and the performance 'shoulds.' You went back and asked the right questions right. So now you believe you have a good idea of what your top CSRs do more, better, and differently to achieve the results that they do, right?"

Bill and Sarah nodded in agreement.

"In contrast, the 'is' is your present reality. It's the way things really are. It's the glaring truth that no one can deny. You already know what your operational 'is' is. Slow response time to incoming calls? That's an 'is.' Less than desired first-call resolution of problems? Another 'is.' High caller abandonment rate? That's an 'is,' too."

"I understand," Bill offered.

"The next issue, then, is your performance reality—your performance 'is.' In order to achieve your performance 'shoulds,' more of your CSRs need to match the performance standards of your top CSRs. You need to determine which of the behaviors exhibited by the top CSRs on a routine basis are the most important to target in the rest of your CSRs. The other CSRs may already be succeeding at some of these practices, so they would not need training in every area."

"Now I really understand," Bill said, excitement evident in his voice. "While the gap is the difference between the 'should be' and the 'is,' there may not be gaps in all twelve key behaviors. So we may not need to address every area."

"You've got it, Bill! As it says on the card, 'The "is" is where the gap is.' But you shouldn't assume that all twelve of the behaviors have gaps and need your attention."

"Our task, then, is to figure out exactly where the gaps are," Sarah observed.

"Yes!" Mike responded. "I imagine your boss's objection centered on the fact that it makes little sense to train a whole slew of people in those areas in which they don't really need training or in which training would not affect results. By suggesting training to your boss, you were jumping to a solution—an expensive one at that. Instead you need to compare the 'is' performance to the 'should be' performance to determine where the gaps are."

"Sounds like we need to go back to the office and ask some of our more typical CSRs how they do with regard to the twelve practices," Bill surmised.

"That's right," Mike agreed. "That's a key part of analyzing the 'is.' You have to get inside every gap and find out why it's there."

"How do we go about doing that?"

"For starters I'd consider focus groups made up of your typical performers. Get inside their heads and ask them to tell you what they do day to day. Ask them which of the ideal behaviors exhibited by the top performers are easy to perform—as well as which ones are more difficult. Ask them if they have a sense of how customers are responding to them. Ask them what you and the company could do to help them perform their jobs better. All this will help you analyze the 'is' and why it exists."

"What specific information should we be going after?" Sarah asked.

"I can't tell you for sure what will work in your business, but I'll give you the basic principles that have worked in mine."

"We're all ears," Sarah offered. "We're obviously open to any help we can get."

Mike dug into his scruffy-looking computer bag. "I'm a chart guy. I love to organize things using diagrams. I call this one The Gap Zapper." He placed a sheet of paper in front of Bill and handed the same sheet to Sarah.

"Let us begin!" he said enthusiastically.

Seven

THE GAP ZAPPER

*B*ill and Sarah stared at the sheets of paper. Mike didn't wait for them to raise their questions; he simply jumped into his explanation.

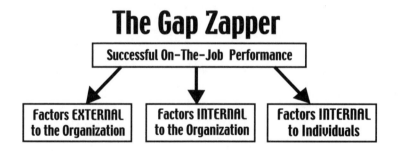

"There are three reasons for performance gaps. One is not under your control, but the other two are."

"Let me guess," Sarah broke in. "The one not under our control is in the box on the left: Factors External to the Organization."

"You got it. That's because those are the things no one in your company has any power to change. Those factors include economic conditions, existing and emerging competition, demographics, taxes, and government regulation."

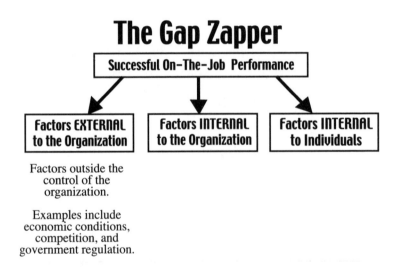

The Gap Zapper

Successful On-The-Job Performance

Factors EXTERNAL to the Organization	Factors INTERNAL to the Organization	Factors INTERNAL to Individuals

Factors outside the control of the organization.

Examples include economic conditions, competition, and government regulation.

"I suppose we could buy out the competition or lobby to lower taxes or relax regulations," Bill suggested.

"True, but for the most part it's better to look at the things you can more readily control. Let's look at the second box: Factors Internal to the Organization. These are the work environment needs. If you'll recall the drawing I did for you on the napkin, work environment needs, along with capability needs, are in the smallest rectangle.

"As a matter of fact, I've carried that napkin with me since the day we met," Bill commented as he pulled it out of his pocket.

"Looks like it's showing some signs of wear," Mike joked.

"Yeah. I should probably have it laminated and framed before it disintegrates."

Mike continued over the laughter: "Okay, back to business! What do you suppose are some of the factors you *can* control in order to close gaps between the 'should' and the 'is' and ensure successful on-the-job performance?"

"We can make sure our employees understand their roles and our expectations," Sarah suggested.

"Excellent!"

"We can provide coaching and give them positive reinforcement," Bill offered.

"Good one. Any other thoughts?"

"Not off the top of my head," Bill admitted.

"Let me add a couple then," said Mike. "You can make certain that effective work systems and processes are in place. You can offer incentives that encourage a higher level of performance. And you can ensure that all employees have access to the information, people, tools, and job aids they need to accomplish their assignments."

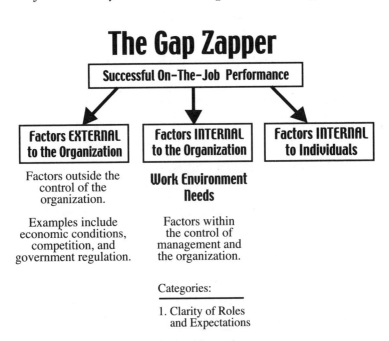

The Gap Zapper

Successful On-The-Job Performance

Factors EXTERNAL to the Organization	Factors INTERNAL to the Organization	Factors INTERNAL to Individuals

Factors outside the control of the organization.

Examples include economic conditions, competition, and government regulation.

Work Environment Needs

Factors within the control of management and the organization.

Categories:

1. Clarity of Roles and Expectations

2. Coaching and Reinforcement

3. Incentives

4. Work Systems and Processes

5. Access to Information, People Tools and Job Aids

"Got it!" Bill said as he scrawled the last note on his Gap Zapper sheet.

"Only one category to go: Factors Internal to Individuals. These are the capability needs," Mike suggested. "Any idea what I mean by that?"

"We have to hire good people," Sarah suggested from her HR perspective.

"Right. What else?" Mike asked as Bill began to make a list under the right box.

"I imagine she means that the individuals in the organization must be qualified to do their jobs," Bill offered.

"Exactly! They must possess specific skills and appropriate knowledge in order to attain successful on-the-job performance."

"Isn't that a function of training?" Bill asked.

"Partly," Mike agreed. "And, of course, big chunks of the skill and knowledge could be the result of education acquired prior to hiring—college, technical school, correspondence courses, and so on. Remember how I told you that the most qualified golf course superintendents are often graduates of turf programs?"

"Sure do," Bill replied.

"There's a bit more to it, though. The other important key is that individuals must have some set of inherent capabilities. An individual who has limited hand-eye coordination or lacks running speed or a sense of balance is unlikely to become a professional athlete."

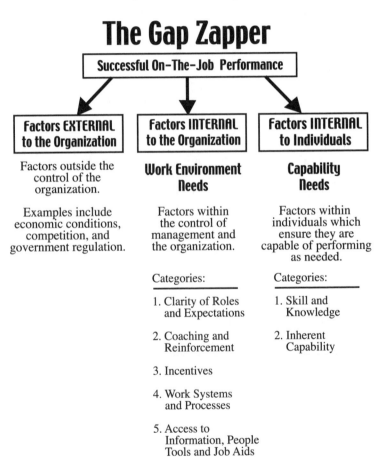

The Gap Zapper

Successful On–The–Job Performance

Factors EXTERNAL to the Organization	Factors INTERNAL to the Organization	Factors INTERNAL to Individuals
Factors outside the control of the organization.	**Work Environment Needs**	**Capability Needs**
Examples include economic conditions, competition, and government regulation.	Factors within the control of management and the organization.	Factors within individuals which ensure they are capable of performing as needed.
	Categories:	Categories:
	1. Clarity of Roles and Expectations	1. Skill and Knowledge
	2. Coaching and Reinforcement	2. Inherent Capability
	3. Incentives	
	4. Work Systems and Processes	
	5. Access to Information, People Tools and Job Aids	

Bill and Sarah made notes under the heading "Factors Internal to Individuals" as Mike continued. "Here's a simple example: I have to have employees who are fluent in Spanish in order to serve my Hispanic customers. That's why *yo hablo español!*"

Bill's face brightened. "I know what you mean. It's been very helpful for me to learn Spanish, too. I've made friends I might not have met otherwise. An added plus is that I know what I'm ordering when I eat at an authentic Mexican restaurant!"

Mike was still chuckling over Bill's comment when Sarah said, "Obviously, inherent capabilities are the things we would look for in the interviewing process before we hire an individual."

"Right," Mike confirmed.

"So then one key," she continued, "is to do a more careful job of describing the inherent capabilities we need. In going for the win, we have to analyze the 'is' of the applicants to determine if there's a gap that would prevent them from ever moving into the 'should' category."

"That's correct," Mike agreed, "but remember that in many cases the gaps you uncover in applicants can be zapped. You don't necessarily have to reject them simply because their 'is' abilities and behaviors are not precisely what you need. It will require a great deal of skill on your part to determine if the applicant has what it takes to progress from 'is' to 'should.' You will have to analyze their 'is' very accurately."

"Wow!" Bill exclaimed as he continued to write. "That's a lot to consider. I don't know if we've ever taken a cohesive look at all that."

"Don't feel bad if you haven't," Mike said encouragingly. "Most companies hire good people and then cut them loose to flounder in unfriendly seas. It took me a long time to put these thoughts together and apply them in my business."

Bill studied his notes. "I see some things we can change right now."

"Hold your horses," cautioned Mike. "It sounds like you want to jump to solutions again."

Once more Mike peered into his shirt pocket, pulled out two green cards, and handed them to Sarah and Bill. This card read:

Jumping to Solutions?

Don't fall for it!

They read the card in silence, then laughed in unison. "I think from now on we're going to look before we leap!" Bill promised.

*B*ill and Sarah left their lunch meeting determined to apply the new information they had gleaned from Mike. They both had some open time at 3:30 that day and agreed to meet in Bill's office.

"I concur with Mike that focus groups are the best way to obtain 'is' and 'should' information. The participants will feed off one another, and we'll get to some meaningful discussions much more quickly," Sarah proposed.

"You're right, but this is going to be a money issue, and it will be far more costly than the two-on-one lunches we had. We're going to have to get Angie's approval."

"Let's get going on our proposal then."

Bill balked. "You know I hate meeting with her. . . ."

"Bill, she's just doing her job."

"So were the lions in the Colosseum."

"Come on! She's not *that* bad!"

*B*y now Angie knew that Sarah and Bill would be precisely on time for their meeting, so she greeted them at her door.

"I love punctuality," she said. "It demonstrates that you're serious about what you're doing."

"Oh, we're serious, all right!" Bill commented while glancing at Sarah.

Angie's first question was "Are you making any progress?"

Yes, no thanks to you! Bill muttered inside himself.

"Yes, we believe we are," Sarah replied.

"Okay, give it to me."

Don't go there, Bill.

Sarah was the one to answer. "We believe the best way to determine what skills and behaviors our typical CSRs lack in comparison to our top performers is to conduct a series of focus groups with them. Because we believe we know what the top CSRs do that makes them successful, we can elicit some ideas that will enable us to zero in on the most crucial performance shortfalls of the typical CSRs."

"Focus groups, huh?" was all Angie said in response.

Bill put his private thoughts aside and joined the discussion. "As you pointed out, there is no valid reason to train all our employees in all the success behaviors if those behaviors aren't crucial to heightened performance or if they're not lacking in all the employees."

"Yes, that's essentially what I said."

"We'd like to get started right away," Sarah added.

"Do you have any idea what this project would cost?"

Here we go with the money thing again. You'd think I work for a lemonade stand, Bill ranted inside.

"We estimate that it will cost no more than two thousand dollars," Sarah responded calmly, knowing full well what was going on in Bill's frustrated mind.

"I can buy that. Go for it."

"Thank you," Sarah and Bill both said.

As they were walking out the door, Angie offered one more thought: "There had better be some solid solutions attached to your findings, though. We're all under a lot of pressure to turn things around here. There's been some slight erosion in our market share, and Corporate isn't going to stand for that."

When they got out of Angie's hearing range, Bill grumbled, "So, heard any good threats lately?"

"Oh, yes, did you hear the one about the two employees who are under a lot of job pressure because the corporate office isn't going to stand for any more erosion in market share?"

"Yeah, I heard that one. It isn't funny."

Eight

MISSING PIECES

We better not mess this up," Bill observed as he and Sarah drew up lists of likely candidates for the focus groups involving typical CSRs.

"You're absolutely right," Sarah agreed.

"Then why is it that I have this gnawing feeling there's something we haven't considered—some important piece of all this that's missing?"

"I have the same feeling," Sarah confessed.

"Maybe there's a management or HR book on this subject."

"Not that I know of. Besides, I don't think we have the time to read books. We have to get the job done."

"That leaves only one alternative."

"Mike, right?"

"Right."

☉

Mike offered to meet with Bill and Sarah during his next large block of available time—two days later. "This could take some time to solve," he told them when they called.

After they had all settled into comfortable chairs in his office, Mike began with a pointed question: "Did any of my suggestions help at all?"

Bill was a bit embarrassed. "I have to confess we haven't conducted the focus groups yet."

"Your boss reject the idea?"

"Actually, she approved the budget for the focus meetings, but, frankly, we're not clear on how analyzing the 'is' is going to lead to solutions. And she's made it very clear that she wants more than data. She expects results."

Mike's next question caught both Bill and Sarah off guard. "You have time to go on a little field trip?"

His inquiry was met by a pair of puzzled expressions.

"Where to?" Sarah finally asked.

"I'm not telling. You'll have to trust me on this one."

They got into Mike's car—actually a large SUV that had seen its share of field duty—and headed toward an East Valley suburb. Mike checked his *Thomas Guide* occasionally to confirm the various exits and turns on the way to his destination.

"Hey, this looks like my neighborhood!" Bill exclaimed.

"It is."

"What are we doing here?"

"You'll see."

A couple of turns later, Mike pulled his SUV into the driveway of an impressive home.

"Hey, this is my house!"

"Yes, it is. You called my field team about a problem you noticed. I thought we'd drive out and take a look. My company is all about quality customer service, remember?"

"How did you know? That I called, I mean."

"I try to keep on top of everything. I don't always succeed, but I try."

They all got out of Mike's SUV, and Bill led them into his expansive, beautifully landscaped backyard.

"Tell me about your problem," said Mike.

"Look at these palm trees," Bill said as he led Mike and Sarah over to a pair of Mexican fan palms.

Bill recalled that they had been planted in that very spot on the same day. They were exactly the same age, the same height, and the same shape when they were transported from Mike's nursery and placed in freshly dug holes in the desert soil.

Yet, as they looked at them, it was obvious that one had thrived while the other had somehow fallen behind. One was tall and sturdy in appearance; the other seemed dwarfed. The difference was striking.

"So what happened?" Bill asked. "Why is the one on the left so much shorter? Why is there such a wide gap?"

"Good question" was Mike's reply. "In order to answer it, we're going to have to get to the root causes."

"You mean it has something to do with the roots?" Bill asked.

"I didn't exactly say that. I'm implying that there could be a number of considerations here. We can't just jump to solutions."

"I understand," said Bill. But he really didn't. It was still a mystery to him.

Mike pressed him. "What do you think the causes could be?"

"I suppose it's possible that one is getting more water than the other, so we need to water them evenly."

"Could be," Mike said as he stooped down to examine the drip system. "But it looks like both of these trees get exactly the same amount of water, unless, of course, one of the drip heads is plugged."

"Maybe one tree gets less sunlight," Sarah suggested. "It could be the shorter tree on the left is shaded by the house during the peak of the day. Maybe Bill needs to have it dug up and planted somewhere else."

"That's a possibility, too," Mike agreed.

"Maybe we need to give the shorter tree more fertilizer" was Bill's next thought.

"I realize I led you on a bit, but do you see what you're doing here?" asked Mike.

"No."

"You're jumping to solutions without looking for root causes. Remember how I told you that what you don't see beneath the greens at the golf course is what actually makes them championship-quality playing surfaces?"

"Yes."

"The same principles apply in your own backyard. True, it could be water or sunshine. They may or may not be factors, so we still need to look for root causes by asking the right questions right. And we need to go to the right sources to ask those questions."

"Meaning?"

"Would you call up the phone company to get help for your palm trees?"

"No."

"How about your cable television service?"

Bill was beginning to see where this was going. "No."

"Great answers. You called my company, and that's why I'm here to help. I'm going to look at things under the surface—the things you can't see."

"Can you explain what you're going to do?" Sarah asked.

"Sure. I'm going to order a soil sample. My team will come out, bore some small holes, and take samples back to the lab. We'll be sure to drill deep enough to find out whether there are rock strata under the struggling tree. We'll check for insects. We'll determine the pH of the soil. We'll test for various nutrients to make sure that both trees have been properly fed. In other words, we're going to ask the right questions right. And we're going to go to the right source—the soil in which these trees were planted. Our goal is very simple: We want to *pin down the causes.*"

"I feel as though I should be taking notes right now," Bill commented.

"No need. Everything I'm explaining to you can be summarized in that easily remembered four-word phrase: 'pin down the causes.' You never, ever jump to solutions. You dig for *causes.* Most times they're not staring you in the face. They're somewhere under the surface."

Mike reached into his pocket and fished out two blue cards. He handed them to Sarah and Bill.

Pin down the causes—

or the causes will pin you down.

"Very clever," Bill responded. "I can see how, in some respects, the causes have pinned us down. We've been struggling to solve our problems without actually digging for the root causes. We know what our 'shoulds' should look like, and we're going to conduct focus groups to uncover and analyze the 'is,' but we still haven't pinned down the causes in order to zap our gaps."

"Bingo!" Mike practically shouted.

"What a mouthful that was, Bill! It sounded like so much bad poetry," Sarah said with a mischievous smile.

"Yeah, I guess it did," Bill replied a bit sheepishly.

"The point is," Mike said, "that I think you're both really getting it, no matter how Bill chose to express it."

"Do you think our typical CSRs can help us pin down the causes?" Bill wondered.

"Absolutely! If you ask the right questions right and really get inside their heads, you'll be amazed at what you will learn."

"I've always believed that our task was to hire qualified people, train them to do their jobs, then cut them loose to do those jobs," Sarah admitted. "But I also believe that people can have an ongoing role in solving problems and enhancing both individual and team performance. People like to be asked for their input—they love to be a part of the process."

"You two are showing amazing progress," Mike lauded. "Ask the right questions in the right way of the right people, and you will be able to analyze the 'is' and pin down the causes. You'll be well on your way to closing the gaps between the 'should' and the 'is.' "

Sarah was pleased with what she had discovered on this field trip. "Mike, I can't begin to tell you how much you've helped us."

When they had returned to Mike's office, Sarah got out of the SUV and turned to her coworker. "Let's go zap some gaps, Bill!"

"You're on!"

Nine

HOCUS, FOCUS

Armed with what they believed was the final answer, Bill and Sarah developed the questions they would use to guide the focus groups. Their objectives were to analyze the 'is' and pin down the causes.

"One thing before we recruit our groups. I think we should try to add a little creativity and build some excitement by calling them something other than focus groups. You know, a theme," Bill suggested.

"Good idea," Sarah agreed. "Any thoughts on names?"

"No."

They both thought for a moment, then Sarah's face brightened. "I've got it! We'll call them 'Bull's-eye Teams' because we're going to aim straight for the target, pin down the causes, and zap the gaps!"

Bill laughed. "That's a stretch for me, but I'll go along with it. Bull's-eye Teams it is."

☉

When they approached the CSRs to seek their involvement, they were again amazed by the level of their enthusiasm. Nearly everyone they asked was willing to participate.

The following Tuesday, Bill and Sarah met with the first group of eight "typical" participants in the small conference room.

"The reason you're here is that we believe no one knows more than you do about customer service and how to make it even better," Bill began. "That's why we asked you to participate in our Bull's-eye Teams."

"The theme for our teams will be 'Zap the Gaps,'" Sarah continued. "As we told you before you signed up, this first meeting will last close to three hours. Then every few months we'll ask you to come together for a shorter meeting so that we can collect any new thoughts and observations you may have."

"Our overall purpose is to discuss any challenges you face on the job, along with your ideas on how to improve our level of service to our customers."

Bill added, "The goal is to give you the opportunity to offer us feedback in a team setting."

"Oh, so it's a focus group," someone piped up from the other end of the conference table.

Bill grinned. "I see you're on to us. We wanted to add a little excitement by adopting a theme. That's why we named them Bull's-eye Teams. But, yes, they're focus groups."

Everyone laughed. Then someone else spoke up. "I don't care what you call them, I'm just glad we'll have an opportunity to speak up. I can already think of several things I'd like to discuss."

"Me, too," another participant called out. Several others nodded or verbalized their agreement.

Sarah and Bill were obviously pleased with the direction in which this was already headed.

Bill again spoke. "We're going to have two Bull's-eye Teams from each shift. Since there's no such thing as a B team at Dyad, we're going to designate the groups from each shift as Team 1 and Team A. But we want to emphasize that this is not a competition. You won't be awarded cash or valuable prizes."

Laughter again rippled through the group.

"We also want you to know that in this meeting there's no such thing as a dumb idea," Sarah added. "You can bring up anything you want, because even though we're technically a focus group, I guarantee that we're not going to stay all that focused. Anything goes."

"The first thing we want to do," Bill said, "is outline the 'shoulds'—in other words, what our numbers should be in terms of response time, first-call resolution, and abandonment rate. These are our target numbers."

Sarah wrote the numbers on a portable white board.

Bill continued: "Now we'll look at the current numbers. These figures represent what our actual performance is, as of last week's report."

Sarah wrote those numbers in a second column, then drew a bold vertical line to separate the two columns. "The differences between the two sets of numbers are our operational gaps. The purpose of putting together Bull's-eye Teams is to identify the causes of the gaps, and then uncover the solutions to zap the gaps."

Bill and Sarah opened the floor to questions and answered them candidly.

Next, they distributed copies of the list of the twelve success behaviors that they had determined through their time with the star performers. They probed deeply to discover how the CSRs were performing in the real world. They asked questions such as "Why do you do it that way?" and "How do you handle this or that?"

Sarah took careful notes throughout the session so that the "is" could be carefully analyzed following the meeting.

It wasn't long before the discussion turned to possible causes of the gaps.

"I have some thoughts on why the operational gaps exist," a young man offered without any hesitation. "I've been thinking about this since you asked me to sign up."

"Go ahead," Bill encouraged.

"Okay, here's the thing. When customers call into Dyad, they simply connect with the next available CSR. If the customer draws a newer CSR, they may have a problem that is beyond the training of that CSR. So then the CSR has to put the customer on hold and figure out who can best help that customer. If the most knowledgeable CSR is on another call, there's a long delay, the customer abandons the call, and the first-call resolution stats go down the tubes."

"Interesting," Sarah ventured. "But you went through intensive training when you were hired. The purpose of the training is to eliminate the gaps between the new hires and the experienced CSRs."

"You just said the magic word," the young man responded. " 'Experienced.' My dad used to say, 'There's no substitute for experience.' I think he was right. Training can give you the facts, but experience helps you apply the facts in different situations."

"Very true," Bill acknowledged as he wrote *Random assignment of calls* on the white board.

Sarah called to mind the last time she had dialed a tech support number about a small problem she was having with her home computer. When she reached the menu, she was prompted to enter several numbers to get to the appropriate CSR. She first pressed 3 to indicate that she was calling about a desktop model rather than a laptop. Then she pressed 5 to denote her particular model. Finally, she pressed 2 to get in line for help on software problems for her particular computer. When she talked to a CSR less than two minutes later, her problem was solved quickly by an obviously experienced individual who had specialized skills in solving her type of problem. Fantastic one-call resolution, she had thought at the time.

"We have another problem along the same lines," a young woman began. "There are some instances where we know the only solution to the customer's problem is to send a field technician to the site of the installation. My customers usually want the service call scheduled while they're on the phone with me. But when I call over to Tech Deployment, I'm sometimes put on hold for ten minutes or more. My customers are forced to listen to our elevator music until I get back online with them. More often than not, they've given up."

"Interesting observation," Bill said as he again wrote on the white board: *Communication problems among various departments.*

"I have a major gripe," a somewhat stern-looking older man said. "I've been here almost since Dyad was started, and so have all our tools. I mean, the computers and software we use are so old that they aren't up to the tasks we face today. They may have been okay three or four years ago, but—"

Bill interrupted him. "Do you have any thoughts on what you'd like to see happen?"

"Sure. Your average kid at home can navigate through huge amounts of information on the Internet quicker than we can get from one screen of information to the next. We lose customers and increase the waiting time because we have to switch from screen to screen, and in the process, the customer's name and other information don't follow along with us while we're doing that. Our own Website for customers is organized better than our internal information. Plus it's easier to use."

"So you're saying, make it easier somehow."

"Yep. That's what I'm saying."

Bill made another note on the board: *Inadequate information systems.*

A relatively new hire confessed, "I hate to admit this, but I still don't know which of the metrics is the most important. Is our goal to resolve problems on the first call, or is it to keep calls short so we can handle more calls? I know I'm measured on all of those things, but I still don't know what the priority is. And I think these goals are somewhat at odds."

"Thank you for that thought," Sarah said.

This sounds like a job for Super Director, thought Bill as he wrote the words: *Unclear expectations.*

An extremely confident young man piped up: "I'd like to know why the heck we even have shift managers. I apologize right now for saying this in front of you, and if you have to fire me, I'll understand. But—*jimminy bugwhack*—they come over, plug into our consoles, listen for a while, unplug, and move on to the next station. They never say anything. They never comment on how we're doing—either good or bad. For all we know they're listening to talk radio on their dang headsets."

Stifled laughter filled the room—and Bill jotted another note on the board: *Managers fail to coach and don't provide feedback.*

As the meeting progressed, ideas kept pouring in. Bill and Sarah were thoroughly impressed by the suggestions offered by the day shift's Team A.

"Do you think there's even any point in conducting the meetings with the other teams? I think we've learned everything we need to know to fix the problems," Sarah suggested.

Bill objected to that idea immediately. "If we relied on what we heard today, we'd be jumping to solutions again. We need to meet with the other teams to discover if they are experiencing the same problems—and how serious these problems really are."

"I guess you're right, Bill," Sarah conceded. "If no one on the other teams mentions these things, they may just be problems in the minds of one or two individuals. But if they are recurring themes, then we have probably pinned down the root causes."

☺

*T*he next day Team 1 gathered in the conference room. The first participant to volunteer said, "My problem is that there's nothing readily available to point me in the right direction. I'm never quite sure what screen to pull up to find the answer, so I kind of wander around sometimes until I find the correct one. There's got to be a better way to connect keywords and phrases to the screens that will offer likely solutions."

"Interesting point," affirmed Bill. He then wrote *Better interface* on the board.

"We could probably use the screens themselves," someone else suggested. "But there are too many of them, there are no clear links between them, and it takes forever to load them. I can load Internet sites at home quicker than I can get into the pages I need at work."

Point taken again! Bill thought as he puzzled over what to write on the board.

Another CSR suggested longer breaks "so I can get refreshed and face another long stretch on the phones."

That'll never fly, thought Sarah. But Bill wrote *Longer breaks* on the board, because, after all, "there's no such thing as a dumb idea."

Someone else spoke up. "I think the problem is that we were hired, given basic training, and then dumped. No one has really followed up with us after the fact."

"How about your managers?" Sarah asked.

"I guess they've helped me understand our products better, and I think I know them fairly well. But I haven't gotten any help on how to deal with irate customers. That's what I really need. I get frustrated pretty easily."

Bill wrote *How to deal with irate callers* on the now-crowded white board.

Bill and Sarah were beginning to notice a certain pattern to the suggestions. A lot of them had to do with efficient access to the right information. Several other comments pointed to the lack of coaching—a problem that needed to be addressed with the shift managers.

Meetings with all six Bull's-eye Teams were completed within a week, and Bill and Sarah decided to get together to sift through and summarize Sarah's notes.

As they walked out of the last meeting, Sarah observed, "We have some really talented people working here."

"Yes, we do," Bill agreed. "And we can thank HR for that!"

☉

*T*he following day Bill sat at his desk and studied the summary he and Sarah had put together. *Some of these suggestions seem so incredibly simple,* he thought, *but others will require a great deal of time and money to research and implement.*

As he studied the lists of ideas again and again, a form of panic welled up inside him. He called Sarah.

"I'm really confused, Sarah. There are so many solutions, and most of them seem valid. How do we know what to do next?"

"Maybe we need to spend some more time with our favorite mentor."

"You're right. I'll give him a call."

Bill made a note of a few of the open times on Sarah's schedule and wasted no time in calling Mike's office. After the usual how-may-I-make-your-life-perfect response from Mike, Bill dug right into the topic of discussion.

"We've really mined a lot of great information from our Bull's-eye Teams."

"What are Bull's-eye Teams?"

"That's what we decided to call our focus groups."

"That's clever! I'm glad it worked out for you!" was Mike's response.

"There's quite an amazing range in the ideas, though," said Bill. "Many of them are quite sound, but we obviously can't implement them all. I'm confused about how to proceed."

"Perhaps we should get together to discuss this," Mike offered.

"My thought exactly!"

⊙

The next morning found Sarah and Bill once again comfortably seated in Mike's office.

"From what you told me on the phone, your teams really came through with quite a few ideas," Mike began.

"They sure did," Bill replied. "Some of the suggestions are so simple that we almost feel a little sheepish about not thinking of them before."

"Do you have an example?"

Bill thought for a moment. "Okay, here's one. Several CSRs said that it takes too long to figure out which screen to launch to access the correct information. One of them suggested a job aid that would serve as a readily available reminder. It's so simple—it's really nothing more than a little printed card or something like that."

Mike grinned. "In the gardening business we would call that 'low-hanging fruit.' "

"Huh?"

"Low-hanging fruit. You know, fruit that you can harvest—pull off the tree—from ground level. You don't need ladders to get to the fruit. These are the easy solutions that you can implement without much effort or expense. It's important to make certain that there are no dangers associated with picking the low-hanging fruit, however. But if you can conclude that there's not a hornet's nest buried in there somewhere, then go ahead and pick it."

"Do you have a term for the more difficult, costly, involved solutions?" Sarah wondered aloud.

"Sure. That's 'cherry-picker fruit.' It's more difficult to reach. You can't stand on ground level and get to it. To harvest this fruit you need more elaborate equipment—a cherry picker mounted on a truck. You get into the basket on the cherry picker and operate hydraulic controls to lift yourself up to the level of the fruit. This is more complex and involves a greater degree of commitment."

"Where do we go from here then?"

"When it comes to cherry-picker fruit, it's absolutely vital that you select the right solutions from the many that were suggested." Mike dug into his shirt pocket and retrieved two purple cards. "This is my last card," he said as he handed copies to his guests, "but I'm very proud of it."

> Sometimes the wrong solution is
>
> worse than no solution.
>
> Select the right solutions!

Mike got right to the point. "What this means is that the solutions you select must match the causes. That's why I warned you against jumping to solutions. If you don't pin down the correct causes, you can't select the right solutions."

"That makes sense," Bill and Sarah both commented.

"Here's an obvious example," Mike continued. "Bill, you had one palm tree in your yard that was shorter than the other, and you didn't like the way that looked. It destroyed your intended symmetry. I could have solved your problem by removing the shorter palm tree and replacing it with one that's the same height as the other one. You'd say, 'Thank you for solving my problem,' and I'd be on my merry way. But if I hadn't pinned down the root causes for the disparity between the two original trees, you could easily have had the same gap again. The new tree could have fallen behind the original tree in growth. It could even have died."

"But you didn't do that," Bill observed. "Instead, you buried some time-release fertilizer or whatever, and you assured me that would help."

"Exactly! My team pinned down the root cause and selected the right solution. By the time the fertilizer has been fully absorbed, both trees should be very close to the same height. With a little monitoring and tweaking, they should remain that way, too."

"Great, Mike," Bill lauded. "I appreciate what you've been doing to pin down the causes of my tree troubles, and Sarah and I are grateful for the wisdom you've imparted to us. Thank you!"

"You're most welcome."

Bill had more to say: "As I've been listening to all the things you've been teaching us, it's become obvious to me that you model all your principles. You truly practice what you preach."

Mike was puzzled. "I'm not sure what you mean by that, Bill."

"I know what he means," Sarah interjected. "He means that you ask open-ended questions—high-yield questions. You don't just tell us what to do. You do all these things yourself. And you help us learn how to do them for ourselves."

"She's right," Bill agreed. "But more than that, you ask probing questions. You dig deep. It's as though you know there are important things under the surface, and you're willing—even eager—to grab the shovel and go for those things."

Mike grinned and replied, "I wasn't even aware that I was doing those things. I don't know if that's my natural instinct or if it's the result of teaching others about gaps. But if my habits have helped you, I'm glad."

Bill and Sarah thanked Mike again and, armed with his advice and encouragement and their new purple cards, they headed back to the office, confident that they could indeed *select the right solutions.*

Ten

FROM CAUSE TO SOLUTION

Over the next few days Bill and Sarah decided to pick as much low-hanging fruit as they could—but only the solutions they were confident would not be harmful. One of the simple ideas they implemented right away was to create a job aid—a laser-printed card that CSRs could tape to their monitors to use as a quick-reference tool. Another idea was to program the function keys on the keyboard to perform specialized shortcuts. Even if these things didn't totally solve the problems, they were not risking much in terms of time or expense—and they were demonstrating their responsiveness to the CSRs' suggestions.

Next, Bill and Sarah turned their attention to those causes that are more difficult to zap. They went after the cherry-picker fruit.

"I believe we've pinned down a variety of causes, but we have more than we can work on," Bill lamented.

"Why don't we follow up with all our CSRs and survey them?" Sarah suggested.

"That seems pointless to me," objected Bill.

"Not really. It's clear we can't deal with all the causes, so we have to prioritize. By taking a survey of all the CSRs, we'll be able to determine which causes have the most impact on performance."

"It'll take too long. We're under the gun to produce results, Sarah. We have to take action, not wait around for the results of more research."

"I understand, Bill, but what if I told you I could have the results in forty-eight hours?"

"I could buy into it then. But how do you propose to accomplish that?"

"We'll send it to everyone by E-mail. It'll be returned by E-mail. The subject line will read 'CSRs: Make Your Life Better!' "

Bill agreed, and they prepared an electronic survey that asked pointed questions about the various causes of gaps that had been uncovered in team meetings. They distributed the questionnaire to all the CSRs by E-mail and requested turnaround within forty-eight hours.

Nearly every CSR came through within the suggested time frame, so they began to compile the data—not all that scientifically, but still carefully enough for it to be of real benefit.

"I can't believe what we've learned from this survey," Sarah commented as she pored over the findings. "This confirms some of the key discoveries we made in the team meetings."

"The most serious cause affecting successful on-the-job performance seems to fall under the heading of 'Factors Internal to the Organization'—that being, of course, the need to make more and better information available to the CSRs," Bill noted. "That would naturally result in improved first-call resolution."

"Right," Sarah agreed. "And another key is to make sure that information is quickly accessible. Rapid access means shorter calls, reduced abandonment rate, and, naturally, faster response time when it comes to new incoming calls."

"Great! We've not only pinned down the causes, but we've also prioritized them. Now how do we harvest the cherry-picker fruit without pumping huge amounts of money into systems? I talked to one of our top developers, and she said that a redesign of the whole software system to enable juggling data screens would run at least a million and a half dollars."

"Maybe we can accomplish the same thing without new software," Sarah ventured. "Maybe we can design an internal Web-style site, import all the data from the current system, and build a search engine into it. We'll ask the CSRs to do what home users do when they get on the Internet—create a list of favorite pages in the Web browser so they can set up their screens in the most useful way."

"But three or more CSRs use each computer," Bill reminded her.

"That's no problem. They could all have their own log-in names so their own list of favorite pages shows up when they sign on."

"I guess that could work," Bill conceded. "But I imagine it would still cost hundreds of thousands of dollars to create the intranet site."

Sarah thought about the problem for a moment, then her face brightened. "I've been chatting with a guy at my health club whose small company develops leading-edge Websites and other information-handling processes. He's been trying to get on our preferred vendor list for over two years, but the IT department never seems to have a project that fits his specialized skills. Maybe if he came in with this plan—and a competitive price to match—he could get his foot in the door."

Bill was skeptical. "Our IT people would need a lot of assurances and references before they'd allow a new vendor access to our systems."

"This guy has great references, though. Fortune 500 stuff. And the thing is, he mentioned to me last week that things have been kind of slow. He's even been forced to do layoffs. So the timing might be just right."

"Do you think Angie would buy it?"

"Only if we can make a business case for it and demonstrate that the investment would offer value and result in far greater returns to the division."

"Let's get to work then!"

"Before we do that, how about running the idea by the IT people and our CSR teams to see what they have to say."

☉

The idea was a hit with the CSRs, Sarah's friend jumped at the chance to build the site, and Angie, in fact, *did* buy it. The people in the information systems department reviewed some of the work done by Sarah's contact and quickly concluded that they were comfortable with his expertise. There were a few holdouts in the department who didn't relish turning their turf over to an outside vendor, but existing workload considerations prevailed and they ultimately went along with the idea.

Perhaps one of the biggest changes, though, was in the way phones were answered. The high cost of a new telecommunications system had long been a roadblock, but thanks to falling prices, a new system became feasible. Angie readily recognized the advantages and authorized the needed funds. Rather than being placed in a general queue, callers would now be asked to listen to a range of options, then press a certain number on their phones to access the CSR in the best position to answer their specific questions. The simplest calls would continue to be channeled to the new hires.

Changing the phone system had another positive effect. Shift managers no longer had to take over difficult calls from inexperienced CSRs because the most difficult calls were channeled to the top performers. As a result, managers could devote more time to coaching typical performers in order to mold them into stars.

Bill made an important decision, too. He decided to prioritize the metrics. He declared in a policy memo that "first-call resolution comes first," meaning that CSRs would no longer struggle with the conflict between that metric and the need to keep calls short.

The real beauty of the whole process was that as Bill and Sarah presented various causes and proposed the right solutions to Angie, she got actively involved and brought numerous valuable suggestions to the table. For the next several weeks Bill and Sarah crossed their fingers and hoped and prayed for improvements in the Monday morning reports.

They would not be disappointed.

Eleven

GOOD NEWS!

Bill sat down at his desk one Monday morning and picked up the weekly report with some trepidation. Despite all of his and Sarah's efforts, he had no real reason to assume that this report would be any different from all the previous ones, and he knew that their time to zap the gaps was running out.

What's this? he asked himself as he studied the numbers. There, in black and white, was a reason for hope. First-call resolution had improved by 8 percent over the previous week. Eight percent! Response time was still hovering in its usual range and the minimal improvement in the call abandonment rate was no cause for joy, but that first-call resolution number practically had him standing on his desktop and singing "We Are the Champions!"

"I hope it's not a fluke," he said when he called Sarah to revel in the report.

It wasn't. The following week, first-call resolution was up by 12 percent.

One week later there was a noticeable improvement in call response time. Bill was beginning to breathe easier.

When Bill and Sarah arrived at Angie's office the following Monday morning for what they thought was going to be a routine meeting, they were met with loud cheers from the executive committee and the day shift managers. The room was garishly decorated with multi-colored balloons, streamers, and congratulatory signs.

"What's going on?" Bill asked—as if he couldn't guess.

"Bill . . . Sarah . . ." Angie said as she met them and led them over to her desk. "For the first time we've seen improvements in all three of the metrics we targeted. We are extremely proud of you both—for the initiative you showed, for your incredible creativity, and for the way you worked together to make great things happen. Would you care to tell us all how you did it?"

"All I did was hire great people," Sarah said with a grin. "And I tagged along with Bill on an interesting drive. So, Bill, why don't you tell them?"

"There's not all that much to tell," Bill offered, addressing the gathering somewhat timidly. "It began when Angie called me into her office, pointed out the problems that needed solutions, and told me we needed to close the gaps. I enlisted Sarah's help, and we began to look for answers. We ultimately discovered what 'going for the win' means—at least for us.

"First, we looked at our pathetic performance and decided we needed to go for the *'shoulds'*—what we wanted our reality to be.

"Next we had to analyze the *'is'*—the difference between what should be and what the reality actually is. Or was.

"Then we learned that we had to pin down the causes. We knew we had to close the gaps, but we also discovered that in order to do so, we had to dig for the root causes.

"Finally, we determined that we had to select the right solutions. We had jumped to solutions in the past, and that didn't work. In order to actually zap the gaps, we needed to dig carefully and deeply and select the right solutions. They weren't always obvious—they were often under the surface, buried right alongside the root causes."

A broad grin spread over Sarah's face. "I finally get it! GAPS!"

"That's it, Sarah. I even made up my own card that spells it all out." Bill reached into his shirt pocket, pulled out a couple of small white cards, and handed one each to Angie and Sarah. It read:

GO FOR THE "SHOULDS."

ANALYZE THE "IS."

PIN DOWN THE CAUSES.

SELECT THE RIGHT SOLUTIONS.

"That's really something, Bill," Angie commented as she glanced briefly at the card. "How did you come up with this concept?"

"Angie, I have to confess we had some outside help."

"Really? You hired a consultant?"

"Not exactly. Remember when you asked me to play for you in the UMOM Homeless Shelter Golf Tournament last fall?"

"Yes."

"Well, there was this . . . this gardener, I guess you'd call him, in my foursome."

"A gardener, huh?"

"Well, more of a landscaper. In fact, his firm maintains the grounds here at Dyad."

"I see," Angie said as she sat down behind her desk, hit the speakerphone button, and dialed a number. "Hi, there. Mike St. Vincent here. What can I do to make your life perfect?" said the voice over the loudspeaker.

"Dad, it's Angie. You know, I keep telling you that you should turn that GAPS idea of yours into a book. I bet it would help a lot of people. It might even help people here at my company."

Bill and Sarah looked at each other with stunned expressions.

Then they heard Mike's thunderous laugh. "I see you've figured out that I infiltrated your ranks!"

"I didn't make the connection until just now, Dad. But I'm sure glad I asked Bill Ambers to play golf in my place last year."

"He's got a great drive, Angie, so he was a real asset to our foursome. He also has a great attitude about Dyad Technologies. I'm sure he's a real asset to your company, too."

Bill actually blushed at hearing these words.

"He is," Angie said.

Mike continued: "I've really enjoyed sharing the GAPS principles with him and Sarah. They make a great team! I'm pleased that it's worked out."

Angie thanked her dad for his role in the exciting changes that had been taking place, and they said their good-byes. Bill sat in silent disbelief for a moment, then sheepishly admitted, "I had no idea. Not even a hint."

Angie understood. "If you had been looking for a family resemblance, there isn't any. Mom and Dad adopted me when I was four. Mom died when I was nine, and Dad raised me on his own. We've been very close the entire time. He's been my constant mentor—always interested in developing my career. I used to follow him around our yard and dig in dirt to look for 'root causes' as he patiently taught me about GAPS. When I saw how you were beginning to tackle the problems here, your strategies reminded me of his GAPS philosophy."

"I was wondering why Mike was willing to spend so much time with us, and that explains it," Sarah interjected. "I'm sure I'm speaking on Bill's behalf, too, but I'm personally grateful that your dad invested all those hours to help us. He must have known what it would mean to you. You're obviously very special to him."

"I know that. And he's special to me," Angie responded, visibly moved by these events.

Then she turned to the group that had gathered to celebrate. "We've got a great win on the scorecard. But we can't sit back and simply relish our win. We're outstanding performers—every one of us. We have to keep looking forward, probing and pushing for the things that will make us even better. I'm confident that there will be many more victories in the months and years ahead! Let's go for it! Let's zap every gap that comes our way!"

EPILOGUE

We who have passed this story on to you believe that every company, no matter what the product or service it offers and no matter what the conditions of the economy, can zap the gaps and turn in a winning performance—provided the company has a sound business model and fills a real, demonstrated customer demand.

Some companies may struggle more than others, simply because of the nature of the business, the intensity of the competition, or the need to continually develop costly new technologies. The numerous recently failed companies—both dot coms and traditional brick and mortar operations—are clear examples of business models that didn't click. In many cases, the perceived needs didn't exist. In other cases, the needs were more readily met by competitors.

But there are stellar companies out there that make steady or growing profits even in difficult economic times. These companies understand that human performance is key—whether it's expressed through warm greetings offered to customers on the phone, or empowered through training, or achieved through changes in the work environment.

In the case of Dyad Technologies, the numbers continued to improve—gradually but steadily.

The Bull's-eye Teams met on an occasional as-needed basis, and small but important enhancements in systems and procedures were the direct result. Angie, Bill, Sarah, and all the others on the team attributed their ongoing success to the GAPS strategy.

There would be tough times ahead, though. The company developed a software upgrade that was fraught with bugs. Customer Service scrambled to help distraught clients work through the problems.

New problems demand new and imaginative solutions. With Angie's ongoing support, Bill, Sarah, and others on the team took a fresh look at the GAPS formula:

GO FOR THE "SHOULDS."

ANALYZE THE "IS."

PIN DOWN THE CAUSES.

SELECT THE RIGHT SOLUTIONS.

Dyad Technologies boldly made the changes that would build stronger individual and team performance. Angie, Bill, and Sarah banded together to employ the GAPS strategy to ensure the successful on-the-job performance of every team member.

They continually identified and succinctly defined and aligned the needs of their organization—business needs, performance needs, and work environment and capability needs.

They focused on hiring people whose skill sets matched the needs of the company. They sought people who learned quickly and were able to multitask.

They made sure that roles and expectations were clearly understood, that team members were carefully coached and regularly reinforced, and that the incentives offered were truly motivating.

They did everything possible to make certain that work systems and processes were up to speed and that people had free access to information, tools, job aids, and other people.

They monitored the factors over which they had control and modified them as needed—but only after they pinned down the real causes and selected the right solutions.

In short, Angie, Bill, and Sarah went for the win by zapping the gaps—and they succeeded!

ABOUT THE AUTHORS

KEN BLANCHARD is the Chief Spiritual Officer (CSO) of The Ken Blanchard Companies, Inc., a San Diego–based full-service management consulting and training organization, which he founded with his wife, Dr. Marjorie Blanchard, in 1979.

Ken is in high demand as a keynote speaker and has addressed gatherings of numerous Fortune 500 companies as well as leading firms around the world. But it is perhaps as an author that he is best known. He is the coauthor of several international bestselling books, including *The One Minute Manager* (with Spencer Johnson); *Everyone's a Coach* (with Don Schula, former head coach of the Super Bowl Champion Miami Dolphins); *Raving Fans, Gung Ho!,* and *High Five!* (with Sheldon Bowles); and *Leadership by the Book* (with Bill Hybels and Phil Hodges). His books have sold in the millions and have been translated into more than twenty-five languages.

The Blanchards are pleased with the fact that their son, Scott, their daughter, Debbie, and her husband, Humberto, are also active in their business.

Ken and Margie are also the proud grandparents of Kurtis and Kyle, the two wonderful sons of Scott and Chris Blanchard, who live near the Blanchards' hometown of San Diego.

Services Available

Ken Blanchard speaks at conventions and to organizations all over the world. The Ken Blanchard Companies offer extensive training and team-building programs that build on the principles of his bestselling books. In addition, the companies conduct seminars and in-depth consulting in the areas of teamwork, customer service, leadership, performance management, and quality.

Visit the website at www.kenblanchard.com or browse the E-store at www.kenblanchard.com/estore. If this story inspired you to learn more about the GAPS principle, go to www.kenblanchard.com/zapthegaps to download a free audio message from Ken.

For additional information on Ken Blanchard's activities and programs, please contact:

The Ken Blanchard Companies
125 State Place
Escondido, CA 92025
(800) 728-6000 or (760) 489-5005
(760) 489-8407 (fax)

DANA GAINES ROBINSON and **JIM ROBINSON** are the founder and chairman, respectively, of Partners in Change, Inc., a consulting firm formed in 1981. Based in Pittsburgh, Pennsylvania, the firm serves companies around the world. Among their clients are Bank One, First Data Merchant Services, First Union Corporation, The Gillette Company, Johnson Controls, Lenscrafters, and QUALCOMM.

Prior to teaming up on Partners in Change, Dana was an internal Human Resource Development (HRD) professional for several years, and Jim was a Vice President at Development Dimensions International (DDI), where he was the primary architect for its most successful training program, "Interaction Management." This is a developmental program that millions of supervisors and managers around the world have attended.

Both Dana and Jim are frequent speakers at national and international conferences. Dana served on the Board of Directors for ASTD from 1999 to 2001.

Together the Robinsons have coauthored and coedited several books including *Training for Impact, Moving from Training to Performance: A Practical Guidebook,* and the award-winning book *Performance Consulting.* Their books have been translated into Spanish, German, and Chinese. In 1999, ASTD presented Dana and Jim with the award for Distinguished Contribution to Workplace Learning and Performance.

Some of their most special times away from work are those spent with their family, which includes seven very special grandchildren.

Services Available

Partners in Change, Inc., is a recognized leader in the area of performance technology, working with clients to ensure that employee performance is linked to and directly supportive of business goals. The process Jim and Dana Robinson formed, called Performance Consulting, enables organizations, business units, and teams to target and achieve higher performance. This approach is also the basis for the services they provide, including:

• Consultation services to assist teams and organizations to incorporate GAPS techniques into current work practices.

- Consulting with management to identify performance gaps and their causes and develop the solutions needed to close the gaps.

- Skill-building workshops, to build the capability of others to identify and close performance gaps.

For more information about the services that Jim and Dana Robinson provide, please visit their website www.partners-in-change.com or contact:

Partners in Change, Inc.
2547 Washington Road, Suite 720
Pittsburgh, PA 15241
(412) 854-5750
(412) 854-5801 (fax)

If you wish to learn more about *Zap the Gaps!*, visit the website www.zapthegaps.com

*I*f you'd like to know more about UMOM Homeless Shelter Golf Tournament and the New Day Center, a homeless shelter and job training center in Phoenix, Arizona, visit www.UMOM.org.

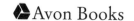

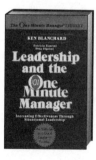